# WHIP IT UP!

# WHIP IT UP!

## OVER 75 FAST, FUN AND EASY RECIPES

### Billy Green

hardie grant books

For my mom, who's always
encouraged me to be me.

# CONTENTS

# INTRODUCTION

Oh, hello there. Thank you for picking up this book and flipping to this page to decide whether or not you want to buy it. Your hair looks great today, by the way. You wanna talk about food?

Ever since I can remember, I've seriously been into food. I've been really into cooking it, reading about it, and now photographing and writing about it. I love how it can trigger memories and take me back to some random time, or help make new traditions/friends/feels. It's kind of this universal bridge that everyone can get into. After all, everyone needs to eat.

When I started my blog back in 2010 it was a way for me to pass the time that wasn't my planned daily schedule between classes with no job. Without fail, every day at 2 pm, it was *Sabrina, the Teenage Witch* for an hour then an episode of *Barefoot Contessa*, then like 30 minutes of me crying inside because I didn't know what to make for dinner. After a full semester of that I took a graphics class and combined that with my photo skills to mock up a newsletter thing that would eventually turn into my blog, *Wit & Vinegar*. a safe place to talk about food and dogs and not wearing pants (trousers, for you British people!) when I'm home. My hope is that all the crazy and weird that happens over there is translated into this book.

Maybe you're new to the whole process of creating food? Great! Welcome, hi – let's cook. All the recipes in this book are fairly simple and can be made by almost anyone. That's half the reason behind the title; the other is that any sort of audio promo can have a whip-crack sound-effect. The whole goal for this book is to get you into the kitchen, playing with your food, and having some fun.

Maybe you're not new to the whole food thing, and that's cool too! Like I said, everything in here is simple but that doesn't mean it's boring. And it also doesn't cost a whole lot to throw one of the recipes together and produce something amazing, and we all love that.

Bottom line is, get in your kitchen right now and cook something. Whip something (it) up! Look for a dish you might have had as a kid and make it into something you'd eat nowadays, or try and make someone's favourite dish and surprise them with it. Don't be afraid! It's a proven fact that when food can smell fear, it just throws up failure in your face. BUT, if that does happen – which, hello, we're all beautiful humans, so it's bound to happen now and again – clean up the failure and try again. It'll make you that much happier with the end result.

So let's turn on some music, get in the kitchen, twerk a little, and make some magic happen...

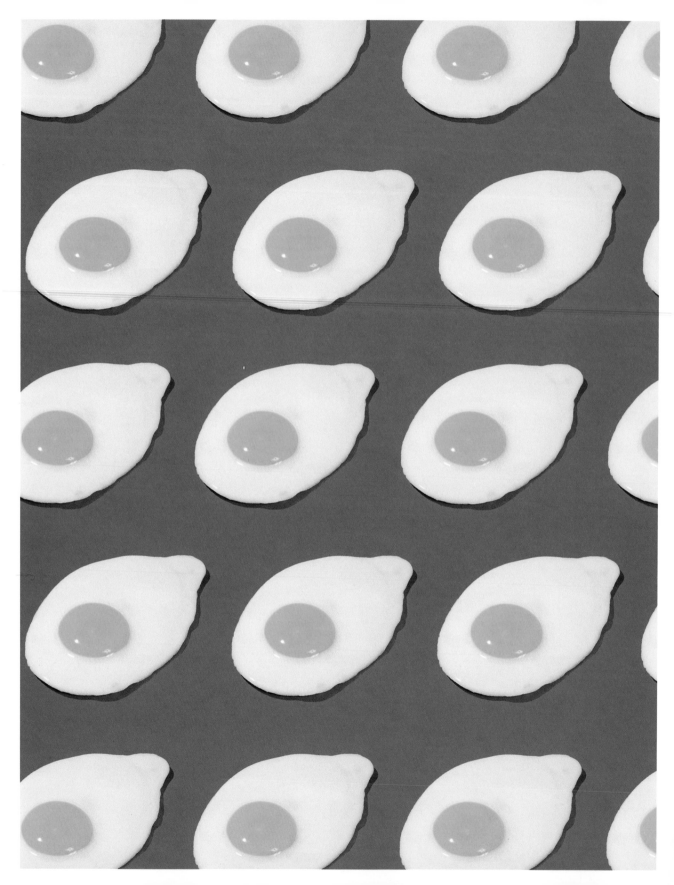

# BREAKFAST

Pretty much all of this chapter revolves around those super-lazy weekend breakfasts where you're eating in bed, possibly binge-watching Netflix and trying your best not to spill syrup all over your pillow. Are all-day pyjamas involved? Maybe. These recipes also work really well with the situation that is brunch – they will impress and comfort everyone.

~~~~~~~~~~~~~~~~~~~~~~~~~~~~~~~~~~~~~~~~~~

# RICOTTA WAFFLES

## SERVES 4

~~~~~~~~~~~~~~~~~~~~~~~~~~~~~~~~~~~~~~~~~~

*Waffles are one of those essential dishes to have in your playbook. Everyone loves them and it's something you can make even more special with just about any topping. These babies are laced with ricotta cheese to give an almost creamy texture, while the addition of cornflour helps with that must-have crispy exterior. You could easily serve these with pure maple syrup and a sprinkle of sea salt, but these go extremely well with some of the Vanilla Strawberry Sauce on page 140 or the Blackberry Bourbon Sauce on page 141 and maybe (definitely) a scoop of Vanilla Buttermilk Ice Cream (page 147).*

220 g (1¾ cups) plain (all-purpose) flour

30 g (¼ cup) cornflour (cornstarch)

3 tablespoons sugar

1 tablespoon baking powder

½ teaspoon bicarbonate of soda
    (baking soda)

½ teaspoon sea salt (or coarse
    kosher salt)

125 g (½ cup) unsalted butter

250 g (1 cup) ricotta

240 ml (1 cup) water

2 large eggs

2 teaspoons pure vanilla extract

Turn on the waffle iron and preheat the oven to 90°C (200°F/Gas ¼), then line a baking sheet and place that in the warm oven. We're creating a nice place for the waffles to hang out so they stay warm and crisp.

In a large bowl, whisk together the flour, cornflour, sugar, baking powder, baking soda, and salt.

Melt the butter in the microwave or a small pan on the stove. Meanwhile, combine the ricotta and water in a large (at least 1 litre/4 cup) measuring cup. As soon as the butter's melted, mix it into the ricotta–water mixture. Beat in the eggs and vanilla, then add that to the dry ingredients. Carefully mix just until it's combined, being careful not to overmix.

Cook according to the manufacturer's instructions on the waffle iron and transfer to the baking sheet in the warm oven. DO NOT STACK WAFFLES BEFORE SERVING unless you want a hot soggy mess. Serve with pure maple syrup and flaky sea salt, or anything else your heart desires.

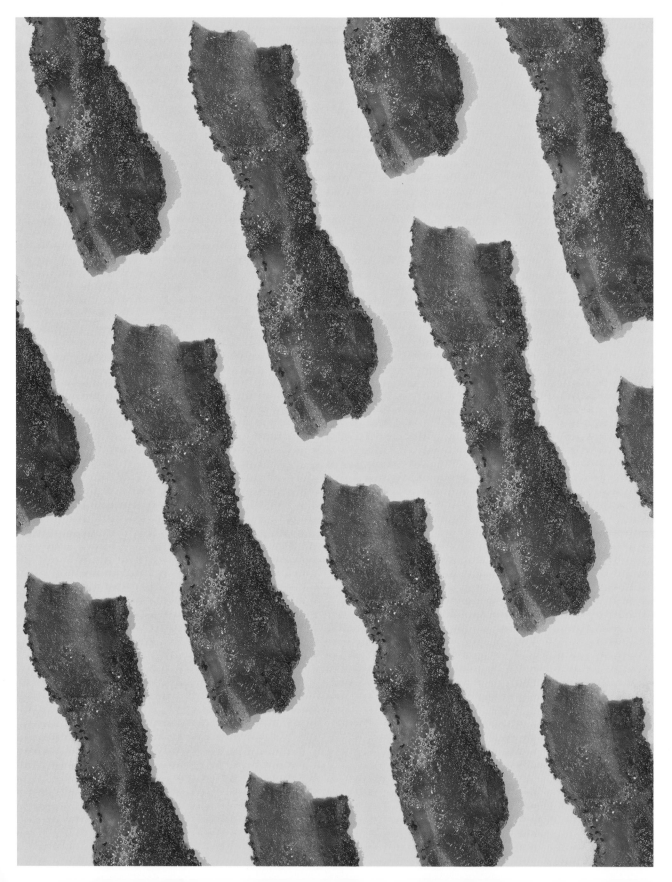

# FAT, FLUFFY PANCAKES

## MAKES 6 PANCAKES

*I find it kind of rare to find someone who doesn't like pancakes. Maybe it's because I have the natural instinct to stay as far away as possible from that crowd, but 9 times out of 10 people will say yes. This is a simple recipe to make super fluffy pancakes to top with whatever the hell you want. Go with your pancake wants and needs.*

125 g (1 cup) plain (all-purpose) flour

2 teaspoons baking powder

¼ teaspoon bicarbonate of soda
(baking soda)

2 tablespoons white granulated sugar

pinch of salt

120 ml (½ cup) buttermilk

50 ml (¼ cup) water

1 large egg

2 tablespoons melted butter or
vegetable oil

½ teaspoon pure vanilla extract

In a medium-sized bowl whisk together the flour, baking powder, baking soda, sugar, and salt.

In a measuring jug, measure out the buttermilk, then the water. Add the egg, butter or oil, and vanilla.

Add the wet mixture to the dry and mix just until there's no visible flour. DO NOT OVERMIX: that leads to flat, tough, chewy pancakes. That's the opposite of fat, fluffy.

Heat up a non-stick frying pan over a medium heat and pour in 3–4 tablespoons of batter. Cook until you see bubbles form around the edge, about 1–2 minutes, then flip over and cook for a minute or so, until golden brown. Make sure your heat isn't too high or the outside will brown before the inside gets a chance to cook.

You can serve these with whatever you want, but here's my two cents: top with bananas and dulce de leche, strawberries and whipped cream, or warm maple syrup and flaky sea salt.

If you want to add anything like blueberries or chocolate chips, then add them right after you pour the batter into the pan. Just toss 4 or 5 pieces, then flip when you see the bubbles and cook like you normally would.

# LOADED BAKED POTATO HASH

## SERVES 3–4

*When I have a weekend breakfast it's usually pretty close to lunch time so there needs to be a good layover for the rest of the day and no hangry episodes before dinner. This hash is perfect for that. I use cold leftover baked potatoes that just need to be chopped up and browned in the pan with the onions and garlic. What makes this business extra special is the loaded part where we make sour cream and bacon acceptable breakfast fare. If you aren't feeling that aspect, toss it out and add whatever vegetables you want: top it with cheese, maybe an egg; follow your breakfast heart.*

3 baked and cooled potatoes*

225 g (½ lb) thick-cut good-quality bacon

1 medium onion, chopped

3 garlic cloves, minced

sour cream, to serve

grated Cheddar cheese, to serve

thinly sliced spring onions (scallions),
    to serve

dash of hot sauce

sea salt and freshly ground black pepper

* For the perfect baked potato, scrub clean 3 large Maris Piper (or russet) potatoes, poke a few times with the tines of a fork and lightly rub with vegetable oil. Roast on a baking sheet at 180°C (350°F/Gas 4) for 1 hour. It's important the potatoes are cooled completely, preferably refrigerated, before using them for this hash. If they're too warm or freshly baked they tend to fall apart too easily.

Chop up the potatoes into roughly 2½ cm (1 in) pieces and set aside.

Cook the bacon strips in a large pan until they're nice and crispy, remove, and set aside on some paper towels. Drain all but 2 tablespoons of the fat.

Cook the onion in the bacon fat over a medium heat until soft and translucent, about 5–7 minutes, then add the garlic and cook for about a minute more, until nice and fragrant. Add in the potatoes, season with salt and pepper, and cook until the potatoes are nice and golden brown and warmed through.

Serve the hash topped with sour cream, grated Cheddar, spring onions, hot sauce, and that bacon all crumbled up. Season and devour.

# CHOCOLATE ORANGE MINI SCONES

## MAKES 25 SMALL SCONES

*These buttery scones help make it okay to eat chocolate for breakfast. They are definitely a biscuit-scone hybrid, and spend no time in chalky Sconeland. If orange isn't your thing, leave it out and try the vanilla.*

250 g (2 cups) plain (all-purpose) flour

1 tablespoon baking powder

½ teaspoon sea salt (or coarse
     kosher salt)

3 tablespoons white granulated sugar

zest of 1 orange (or the scraped seeds of
     a vanilla pod)

110 g (1 stick) cold unsalted butter

120 ml (½ cup) buttermilk, plus
     2 tablespoons for brushing tops

½ teaspoon pure vanilla extract

100 g (3½ oz) good-quality dark
     (bittersweet) chocolate, chopped

optional: demerara (turbinado) sugar,
     for sprinkling (optional)

In a large bowl whisk together the flour, baking powder, salt, sugar, and zest or vanilla. Use the large holes on a box grater to grate the cold butter into the dry ingredients, then quickly use your hands to mix it in and slightly break it up. Place the bowl in the freezer.

In a small bowl, add the buttermilk and vanilla extract and beat with a fork. Remove the mixture from the freezer and quickly incorporate the wet ingredients into it. Once it's almost fully combined, add the chocolate. Use your hands to knead the dough a couple of times – it shouldn't be sticky or too dry, but just combined.

Next, using a 23 x 23 cm (9 x 9 in) cake tin or pie dish, pat out the dough evenly – I find this easier than trying to gather the dough on a cutting board. Using a 4–5 cm (1½–2 in) round biscuit cutter, cut out the scones, pushing straight down – never twisting – and cutting as close as you can to the previous. Once you can't cut anymore, carefully gather the scraps, pat into the same 2 cm (¾ in) thickness and cut out a few more scones. Don't try and use the rest of the scraps – the scone will turn out tough.

Place the scones on a large baking sheet lined with baking parchment and place it in the fridge or freezer to help chill the butter while you preheat the oven to 200°C (400°F/Gas 6). Once the oven is preheated, brush the tops of the scones with the 2 tablespoons of buttermilk and lightly sprinkle with the demerara sugar if you choose. Bake for 10–12 minutes, until lightly golden brown.

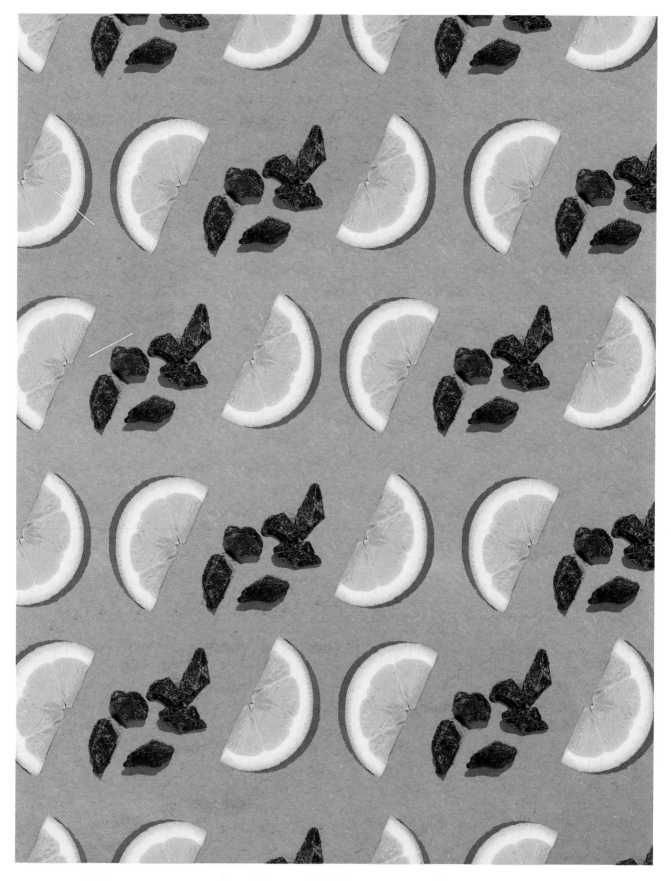

# EGGS IN SRIRACHATORY

## SERVES 4

*When I was initially testing this I was visiting my mom and we ended up 'testing' it about 4 days in a row – it's that good. This is a slight spin on the classic eggs in purgatory where we go ahead and just use Sriracha to give it that kick with a little extra flavour. The sauce can easily be made at least a day ahead and it's also a perfect excuse for carbs, using good crusty bread as a tomato and yolk boat.*

2 tablespoons olive oil

1 medium onion, chopped

3 garlic cloves, minced

2 × 400 g (1 × 28 oz) tins chopped
    tomatoes

2–3 teaspoons Sriracha

sea salt and freshly ground black pepper

4–5 eggs

Lancashire cheese (or queso fresco),
    crumbled, for serving

freshly chopped coriander (cilantro), for
    serving

crusty bread, for serving

Preheat your oven to 180°C (350°F/Gas 4).

In a large frying pan (one you have a lid for), heat the oil and sauté the onion until soft and translucent, about 5–7 minutes. Add the garlic and cook for 1–2 minutes until fragrant. Stir in the chopped tomatoes and Sriracha and season to taste. Bring to a simmer, and cook for 10 minutes.

Make 4 dents in the sauce and crack the eggs into each dent, or go ahead and portion the sauce between 4 ramekins then make that dent and drop the eggs in those. Bake for 10–12 minutes until the whites are just barely set and the yolks are still money golden runny.

Top with the crumbled cheese and fresh coriander, and serve with crusty bread.

# BROWNIE GRANOLA

## MAKES ABOUT 650 G (4 CUPS)

*Sometimes my main goal for breakfast is to see how I can pretend a dessert is somewhat healthy enough to wake up to. Enter brownie granola. It's not overly sweet or chocolatey, but it's just enough to make me think for a second that I'm having crunchy bits of brownie for breakfast.*

250 g (2½ cups) oats

125 g (1 cup) roughly chopped walnuts

40 g (⅓ cup) cocoa powder

80 ml (⅓ cup) vegetable or coconut oil

4 tablespoons honey

70 g (⅓ cup) light brown sugar

½ teaspoon sea salt (or coarse
    kosher salt)

50 g (2 oz) chopped dark (bittersweet)
    chocolate

Preheat your oven to 150°C (300°F/Gas 2) and line your largest baking sheet with baking parchment.

In a large bowl, mix together the oats and walnuts. Heat the cocoa powder, oil, honey, brown sugar, and salt in a small saucepan for 3–5 minutes until heated through and you just start to see bubbles.

Use a rubber spatula to mix the sticky mess into the oat and walnut mixture. Spread out onto the baking sheet and bake for 10 minutes. Give everything a good stir, bake for another 10 minutes, mix again, and bake for a final 10 minutes. Remove from the oven and scatter the chocolate all over the top. It'll start to melt immediately so there's no second scattering. Let cool completely before devouring or moving to an airtight container, where it will keep for a week.

# CHOOSE YOUR OWN ADVENTURE BREAKFAST ROLL

## MAKES 12 ROLLS

*Everybody knows the the classy thing to do with any brunch invite is to show up with a pan of fresh cinnamon rolls. What if I told you, though, that you could put something else besides butter, cinnamon, and sugar in there and really blow people's hair back? Of course I'm still telling you about cinnamon rolls, because it's a necessary life skill, but I've got a few extra goodies for you. The important thing is that you figure out how to master the sweet dough – then you can fill the inside void with all your dreams.*

60 ml (¼ cup) water

7 g (¼ oz) sachet active dried yeast

125 g (½ cup) unsalted butter

185 ml (¾ cup) buttermilk

½ teaspoon salt

1 egg

50 g (¼ cup) white granulated sugar

400 g (3½ cups) plain (all-purpose) flour

Turn on your oven to the lowest setting: even the warm setting is fine – we're just creating a makeshift proof box.

Next, make sure your water is the right temperature – if it's not correct you'll kill the yeast. Use a thermometer and heat up the water between 38–43°C (100–110°F), or whatever the temperature on the packet of yeast says. Sprinkle the yeast over the water and carefully mix it in. Let this sit for about 10 minutes.

In a small saucepan, melt the butter. Remove from the heat and add the buttermilk. Set aside.

In a large heatproof bowl mix together the salt, egg, and sugar. Mix in the butter–buttermilk mixture, then add 250 g (2 cups) of the flour and mix until it's all combined. Check your yeast to see if there are little bubbles or any form of life. It should be all bloomed so add it to the flour mixture along with the remaining flour. Mix until the spoon's not really doing its job, then use your hands to finish kneading it all together for another minute or so.

Turn off your oven and cover the bowl loosely with cling film (plastic wrap) and place inside for 1–1½ hours, until the dough has doubled. Roll out the dough into a rough 30 x 43 cm (12 x 17 in) rectangle. I either do this on a floured cutting board or flip over a large baking sheet, flour it, and use it as a guide to roll out on. Now for the adventure to begin, turn to the next two pages.

# CINNAMON ROLLS

*To me, the perfect cinnamon roll is gooey inside, studded with pecans, and topped with some sort of tangy glaze. If you're more partial to an icing (frosting), use the filling from the Celebration Cake (on page 119).*

50 g (2 oz) unsalted butter, melted

150 g (¾ cup) light brown sugar

1 tablespoon cinnamon

200 g (½ cup) pecans

### For the icing

155 g (1¼ cups) icing (confectioners')
    sugar

2 tablespoons whole (full-fat) milk

80 g (3 oz) cream cheese, softened

2 tablespoons unsalted butter, softened

½ teaspoon pure vanilla extract

pinch of salt

Grease a 23 × 33 cm (9 × 13 in) baking sheet and set aside.

In a small bowl mix together the melted butter, brown sugar, and cinnamon. Smear that evenly over the rectangle of dough you've created and sprinkle with the pecans. Carefully roll up, starting from one long end of the rectangle until you've got a long log of dough. Slice this into 12 even rolls using a serrated knife (using light pressure and a back-and-forth sawing motion). Cut off the knobby ends, cut the log in half, then each half into thirds, then each third in half. Carefully transfer slices to the baking sheet; you should have 4 rows of 3.

Lightly cover with cling film (plastic wrap) and prove for another 45 minutes. After 30 minutes start to preheat the oven to 180°C (350°F/Gas 4), then once the 45 minutes is up remove the cling film and bake for 20–30 minutes, until golden brown.

Make the icing by beating together the rest of the ingredients until smooth and fluffy. Let the cinnamon rolls cool, about 15 minutes, before spreading the icing all over da place.

# STICKY BUNS

*This really isn't a recipe as much as it is an alternative to those cinnamon rolls.*

1 batch Simple Butterscotch Sauce
    (page 138)

all the ingredients from the Cinnamon
    Rolls above, minus the icing.

Before you make the filling, whip up a batch of Simple Butterscotch Sauce and pour that all over the bottom of the prepared tin. Top with the 200 g (½ cup) of pecans, then continue with the rest of the steps. Instead of making the icing you're going to let the rolls sit for about 10 minutes when they get out of the oven, then flip the pan over onto a serving dish so that gooey butterscotch is now ready for take off.

# ALMOND ROLLS

*This is the hot swirlier American cousin of almond croissants. I just know these are, like, really good and perfect for the cinnamon hater in your life (GET THEM OUT OF IT).*

230 g (8 oz) cream cheese

125 g (1 cup) icing (confectioners') sugar, sifted

1¼ teaspoons almond extract

pinch of salt

60 g (½ cup) sliced almonds

*For the glaze*

125 g (1 cup) icing (confectioners') sugar, sifted

4–6 tablespoons whole (full-fat) milk or double (heavy) cream

¼ teaspoon almond extract

pinch of salt

Beat together everything except the sliced almonds until light and fluffy. Spread the mixture evenly over the rectangle of dough you've created and sprinkle with half the sliced almonds. Carefully roll up, starting from one long end of the rectangle until you've got a long log of dough. Slice this into 12 even rolls using a serrated knife (using light pressure and a back-and-forth sawing motion). Cut off the knobby ends, then cut the log in half, then each half into thirds, then each third in half. Carefully transfer each roll to the baking sheet: you should have 4 rows of 3. Sprinkle with the remaining almonds.

Lightly cover with cling film (plastic wrap) and rise for another 45 minutes. After 30 minutes start to preheat the oven to 180°C (350°F/Gas 4) then once the 30 minutes is up remove the cling film and bake for 20–30 minutes until golden brown. Make the glaze by stirring together all the ingredients and drizzling over da buns about 15 minutes after they come out of the oven. Serve warm.

# NUTELLA ROLLS

*Um, this one's pretty self-explanatory. All the Nutella, all the rolls.*

50 g (2 oz) cream cheese

205 g (⅔ cup) Nutella

icing (confectioners') sugar, to sprinkle on top (optional)

Beat together the cream cheese and Nutella, then smear the mixture evenly over the rectangle of dough. Carefully roll up, starting from one long end of the rectangle until you've got a long log of dough. Slice this into 12 even rolls using a serrated knife (using light pressure and a back-and-forth sawing motion). Cut off the knobby ends, then cut the log in half, then each half into thirds, then each third in half. Transfer each roll to the baking sheet: you should have 4 rows of 3.

Lightly cover with cling film (plastic wrap) and prove for another 45 minutes. After 30 minutes preheat the oven to 180°C (350°F/Gas 4) then once the 45 minutes is up remove the cling film and bake for 20–30 minutes, until golden brown. Top with sugar, if using, and serve warm.

# LEMON ROLLS

*This one has spring written all over it. The flavour is super bright from all the lemon ond sort of creamy from the cream cheese. It's kind of perfect to be honest.*

230 g (8 oz) cream cheese

125 g (1 cup) icing (confectioners') sugar, sifted

zest of 1 lemon

pinch of salt

*For the glaze*

125 g (1 cup) icing (confectioners') sugar, sifted

4–6 teaspoons lemon juice

pinch of salt

Using an electric mixer, beat together everything until light and fluffy. Spread this all over your dough rectangle. Carefully roll up, starting from one long end of the rectangle until you've got a long log of dough. Slice this into 12 even rolls using a serrated knife (using light pressure and a back-and-forth sawing motion). Cut off the knobby ends, then cut the log in half, then each half into thirds, then each third in half. Carefully transfer each roll to the baking sheet: you should have a total of 4 rows of 3.

Lightly cover with cling film (plastic wrap) and prove for another 45 minutes. After 30 minutes preheat the oven to 180°C (350°F/Gas 4) then once the 45 minutes is up remove the cling film and bake for 20–30 minutes, until golden brown.

Let the rolls cool for about 15 minutes. Make the glaze while they cool by mixing all the ingredients together and drizzling it over the top, and serve.

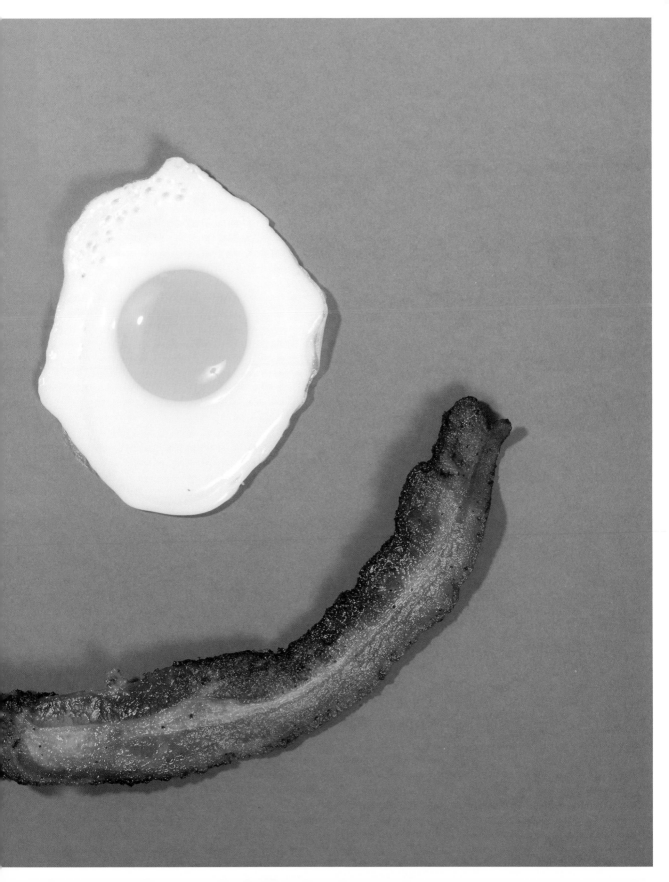

# LUNCH & DINNER

We all know dinner is hard; half the time I don't even know what I'm having. That's where this chapter comes in. Everything is simple, and most of the dishes come from things I had as a kid so we know the comfort factor is like a 10. Even if there are a couple of things that take a little longer, that just gives you more time to pre-game with tortilla chips or a cocktail.

# CORIANDER PESTO

## MAKES ABOUT 250 G (1 CUP)

*I love a good pesto and this one is probably at the top of my list. The salty cotija and the mellow flavour of the coriander are perfect together and I almost always have some in my fridge to just put on a sandwich, or a bowl of pasta or rice. It's a great thing to serve a crowd and that vibrant green wins over anyone. If you can't find the cotija, you can definitely substitute Parmesan, but nothing really matches cotija.*

100 g (2 cups) fresh coriander (cilantro) leaves (you can include some stem if you want)

70 g (⅔ cup) crumbled cotija cheese or Parmesan

1 garlic clove, minced or grated

juice of ½ lime

dash of hot sauce

80 ml (⅓ cup) olive oil

Throw everything except the olive oil into a blender or food processor and blend until chopped. Scrape down the sides, then, with the machine running, drizzle in olive oil and blend until it all comes together. I don't usually add salt because the cotija tends to be pretty salty but if you're using Parmesan, double check and season to taste. It will keep in an airtight container in the fridge for up to 2 weeks.

Now, to put it to use. I've got a pasta dish on the next page and these are some further options for the rest of your life:

Aioli: Mix equal parts pesto and mayonnaise. Use on all your sandwiches, burgers, etc.

Pesto Ranch: Mix together equal parts pesto, sour cream, mayonnaise, and buttermilk.

Pesto Butter: Stir 125 g (½ cup) pesto in with 60 g (¼ cup) of softened butter. Slather on rolls, fresh grilled corn, your face, etc.

# ROASTED CAULIFLOWER & PESTO PENNE

## SERVES 4–6

*This dish is actually a really good winter one when cauliflower is at its peak and you need a giant bowl of carbs. It might sound weird to add cauliflower to pasta, but when it's roasted it gets nice and soft and slightly nutty. It's the perfect complement to the Coriander Pesto (page 43).*

1 medium–size cauliflower

2 tablespoons olive oil

sea salt and freshly ground black pepper

85 g (⅔ cup) chopped walnuts, toasted

450 g (1 lb) penne pasta

1 batch Coriander Pesto (page 43)

a handful of crumbled cotija or grated
    Parmesan cheese, to serve

Preheat your oven to 220°C (425°F/Gas 7) and start to bring a large pot of water to a boil for the pasta.

Chop up the cauliflower head into florets and place on a large baking sheet lined with baking parchment. Drizzle with the olive oil and season with salt and pepper. Toss to combine and roast for 15 minutes until golden brown and softened.

While the cauliflower's roasting, toast the walnuts in a dry frying pan over a medium heat until lightly toasted and smelling fine.

By the time the cauliflower's ready the water should be boiling. Add the pasta and cook according to the time on the package. Drain the pasta, reserving about 250 ml (1 cup) of the pasta water. To the drained pasta add the cauliflower, walnuts, pesto, and about 250 ml (½ cup) of the pasta water. Toss to combine and add more pasta water if the dish seems too dry. Serve topped with crumbled cotija or Parmesan.

# GINGER DIJON BBQ SAUCE

## MAKES ABOUT 240 ML (1 CUP)

*I love a good BBQ sauce. Even better, I love a good BBQ sauce that's got a little something extra happening with it. This sauce has a nice kick from the ginger and Dijon and goes great with a pulled pork or chicken sandwich or maybe even better: pulled pork nachos.*

60 ml (¼ cup) rice wine vinegar

240 ml (1 cup) ketchup

2 tablespoons Dijon mustard

1 teaspoon salt

½ teaspoon black pepper

45 g (¼ cup) light brown sugar

½ teaspoon garlic powder

½ teaspoon onion powder

1 teaspoon grated garlic

Combine all the ingredients and bring to a simmer.

Continue cooking for 15–20 minutes, until it's thickened slightly. Store in an airtight container in the fridge for up to 2 weeks.

# PULLED BBQ CHICKEN SANDWICHES WITH SESAME SLAW

## SERVES 4–6

*I embrace any type of BBQ because it's meat slathered in sauce and I'll never turn that away #teammeat. At home I go the route of braising some chicken thighs, making a quick Ginger Dijon BBQ Sauce, then cramming all that in a sandwich with some slaw. It's a win-win for everyone – unless you don't eat meat...*

*For the pulled chicken*

900 g (2 lb) boneless skinless chicken
   thighs
1 teaspoon sea salt (or coarse kosher salt)
½ teaspoon freshly ground black pepper
1 onion, chopped into quarters
4 garlic cloves
1 quantity of Ginger Dijon BBQ Sauce
   (page 47)

*For the slaw*

1 tablespoon toasted sesame oil
3 tablespoons rice wine vinegar
1 teaspoon sea salt
½ teaspoon white granulated sugar

½ teaspoon freshly ground black pepper
300 g (4 cups) shredded cabbage
1 medium carrot, grated
20 g (⅓ cup) chopped fresh coriander
   (cilantro)
4 spring onions (scallions), thinly sliced

*For assembly*

4–6 good-quality hamburger buns

To make the chicken, combine everything except the BBQ sauce in a large heavy-bottomed saucepan, cover with 5 cm (2 in) water and bring to a boil. Turn down to a simmer and cook for 45 minutes.

While the chicken's cooking make the BBQ sauce by following the recipe on page 47.

To prepare the slaw, combine the sesame oil, rice wine vinegar, salt, sugar, and pepper in a large bowl. Whisk to combine then toss in the rest of the ingredients. Refrigerate until you're ready to eat.

When the chicken's done, remove from the pan and shred using 2 forks. Add the BBQ sauce and toss. To assemble the sandwiches, toast some good-quality buns, then top the bottom bun with pulled chicken and a small mountain of slaw. Finish with the top bun and devour.

# GARLIC MUSUBI FRIED RICE

## SERVES 4

*Spam musubi is a gift from Hawaii that I am forever grateful for: a chunk of rice topped with a crispy piece of Spam, all wrapped in a piece of seaweed – basically Spam sushi. I went and took all that and made it into something I could just eat for dinner in a giant bowl, probably slathered in Sriracha. The furikake (a Japanese seasoning) is really something you should look for – and be prepared to want to put it on everything. I've seen it at a few regular grocery stores, but if you can't find it try an Asian supermarket.*

vegetable oil

½ x 340 g (12 oz) tin Spam, chopped into 1 cm (½ in) dice

2 eggs, lightly beaten

3 garlic cloves, minced

650 g (3½ cups) cold cooked long-grain white rice*

30 g (⅓ cup) thinly sliced spring onions (scallions)

2–3 tablespoons furikake, plus extra to garnish

soy sauce, to serve (optional)

* If you try to use fresh warm rice you'll end up with a mushy mess. This is the perfect time to use up that leftover take-out rice.

Add a splash of vegetable oil to a large frying pan or wok and fry up the Spam, cooking for 3–5 minutes over a medium–high heat, until browned and crispy on all sides, then set aside.

Add a little more oil to the pan if needed then pour in the eggs and the minced garlic and fry the eggs, moving them around the pan quickly so they don't burn. Once cooked, remove and set aside with the Spam.

Splash a little more oil into the pan and add the rice, frying it for just a couple of minutes to warm it up and give it a little colour. Add the Spam and eggs back into the pan and mix, breaking up the eggs if needed.

Once that's all heated, toss in the onion and sprinkle over the furikake. Taste for seasoning and add more furikake if you like. There's already salt in the furikake, but if you feel you really need it then add some soy sauce.

# CALIFORNIA BURGERS

## SERVES 4

*I love all kinds of burgers – #teammeat, remember? – but there's something so California and cool about these. They're dead simple in the ingredients, super fresh, and the tang from the special sauce and the sweetness from the onions makes me just want to eat, like, a thousand. I won't, because I love my heart, but I wouldn't mind making out with a few of them.*

*For the caramelised onions*

2 tablespoons butter

1 large onion, chopped

*For the secret sauce*

60 ml (¼ cup) mayonnaise

2 tablespoons ketchup

1 tablespoon pickle relish

½ teaspoon soy sauce

½ teaspoon white vinegar

½ teaspoon white granulated sugar

¼ teaspoon garlic powder

*For the burger*

450 g (1 lb) minced (ground) beef

sea salt and freshly ground black pepper

your favourite cheese

*For assembly*

4 good-quality hamburger buns

1 beef tomato, sliced

iceberg lettuce

Start out with the caramelised onions. In a large pot melt the butter then add the onions and cook over a low–medium heat, stirring often, until very soft and golden brown, about 30–45 minutes.

Meanwhile, mix the ingredients for the secret sauce (glorified thousand island) in a small bowl and place it in the refrigerator. If you have the option to make it the day before, do so. It gets a little better with that one day.

To make the burger patties, lightly wet your hands and shape the minced beef into tennis-ball sized balls, manhandling them as little as possible. Flatten on the palm of your hand to around 2 cm (¾ in) thick. Season with salt and pepper and let them sit at room temperature for about 20 minutes. If you want to get real freaky you could use the Steak Seasoning from page 194.

Grill the patties for about 2–4 minutes per side. Once you flip them over and let it cook for a minute, top it with cheese then put a lid on the pan. This helps melt the cheese (it's my secret with any burger, and grilled cheese for that matter). Check after a minute or so, and continue to cook until the cheese has fully melted.

After the patties are cooked, let them rest for just a minute while you toast the buns, then you can assemble. Put whatever amount you feel comfortable with: bottom bun, secret sauce, tomato, lettuce, patty, caramelised onions, top bun.

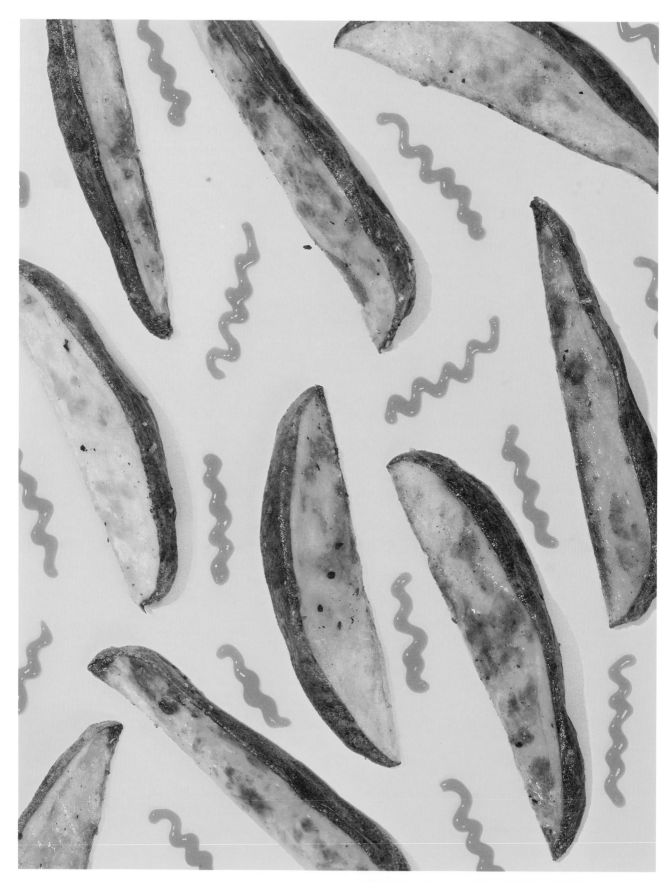

# STEAK-SEASONED STEAK FRIES

## SERVES 4

*I told you that I put steak seasoning on everything. I'm pretty sure there's a law somewhere that says you have to have fries with your burger and I'm adding to that saying they need to be elevated with Steak Seasoning. These guys are great with burgers or pulled pork or a dousing of chilli and cheese, but to keep it simple we're dipping them in a lot of Sriracha ketchup.*

*For the fries*

3 medium Maris Piper (or russet) potatoes

2 tablespoons vegetable oil

1 tablespoon Steak Seasoning (page 194)

*For the Sriracha ketchup*

1 teaspoon Sriracha

120 ml (½ cup) ketchup

Preheat your oven to 200°C (400°F/Gas 6) and line your largest baking sheet with baking parchment.

Cut each potato into 8 wedges and place on the baking sheet. Drizzle with oil, sprinkle with seasoning, and toss to make sure they're evenly coated. Arrange on the baking sheet so they're in a single layer: any overlapping won't get crispy.

While the fries are baking, make the Sriracha ketchup by mixing the two ingredients together and storing in a small container in the fridge.

Bake the fries for 20 minutes, flip, then bake for an additional 20 minutes. Sprinkle with additional Steak Seasoning if you're feeling it, and serve with the Sriracha ketchup.

# BBQ CHICKEN PIZZA

## SERVES 4

*This slice of magic is a huge childhood favourite of mine. A local pizza joint had it on their menu with straight-up BBQ sauce, mozzarella, and chicken. Over the years I've upgraded the toppings a bit, to go from basic to Mariah Carey working out in kitten heels.*

olive oil

½ batch of Easy Pizza Dough (page 198)

120–180 ml (½–¾ cup) of Ginger Dijon BBQ sauce (page 47)

225 g (8 oz) shredded mozzarella

265 g (1½ cups) chopped or shredded cooked chicken

150 g (¾ cup) fresh sweetcorn, right off one cob (absolute dealbreaker without corn)

1 shallot, thinly sliced

25 g (½ cup) chopped fresh coriander (cilantro)

Preheat your oven to 250°C (500°F/Gas 10) and line a large baking sheet with aluminium foil.

Grease the foil with a little olive oil and press out the dough into a rough 28 × 43 cm (11 × 17 in) rectangle. Spread out the sauce on top of the dough, really using as much as you want to make it your level of sauciness. Top with the mozzarella, followed by the chicken, corn, and the shallot. Bake for 10–12 minutes, until it's hot, bubbly, and golden brown.

Let cool for a few minutes then top with the coriander and serve.

# BUFFALO PANZANELLA

## SERVES 4

*This dish is just the greatest because it's kind of a salad made up almost entirely of bread. This is like a dream come true for me. The buffalo we're talking about here is the hot-wing variety, minus the wings, by making a wing sauce vinaigrette and tossing that with the classic additions of celery and blue cheese crumbles.*

*For the vinaigrette*

1 teaspoon Dijon mustard

1 clove garlic, minced

4 tablespoons hot wing sauce

1 tablespoon rice wine vinegar

80 ml (⅓ cup) olive oil

½ teaspoon sea salt (or coarse
kosher salt)

¼ teaspoon freshly ground black pepper

*For the panzanella*

⅓–½ loaf French or sourdough bread,
chopped into 2½ cm (1 in) cubes

2 tablespoons olive oil

sea salt and freshly ground black pepper

1 shallot, thinly sliced

240 g (1½ cups) halved cherry tomatoes

3 stalks celery, sliced, leaves and all

90 g (2 cups) baby rocket (arugula)

100 g (½ cup) blue cheese, crumbled

For the vinaigrette, throw everything into a small jar with a tight-fitting lid and shake until combined. Set aside.

To toast the bread, preheat the oven to 180˚C (350˚F/ Gas 4) and line a large baking sheet with baking parchment.Toss the bread cubes with the olive oil, season with salt and pepper, and bake for 10 minutes, shaking the baking sheet halfway through to mix 'em up. Once they're toasted let them cool for a few minutes while you prep the rest of the ingredients.

To assemble, toss the croutons with the vegetables and blue cheese, then season and toss with the buffalo vinaigrette. Serve right away. If you wanted to take this out for a spin to a picnic, wait to toss the vinaigrette in there until right before serving.

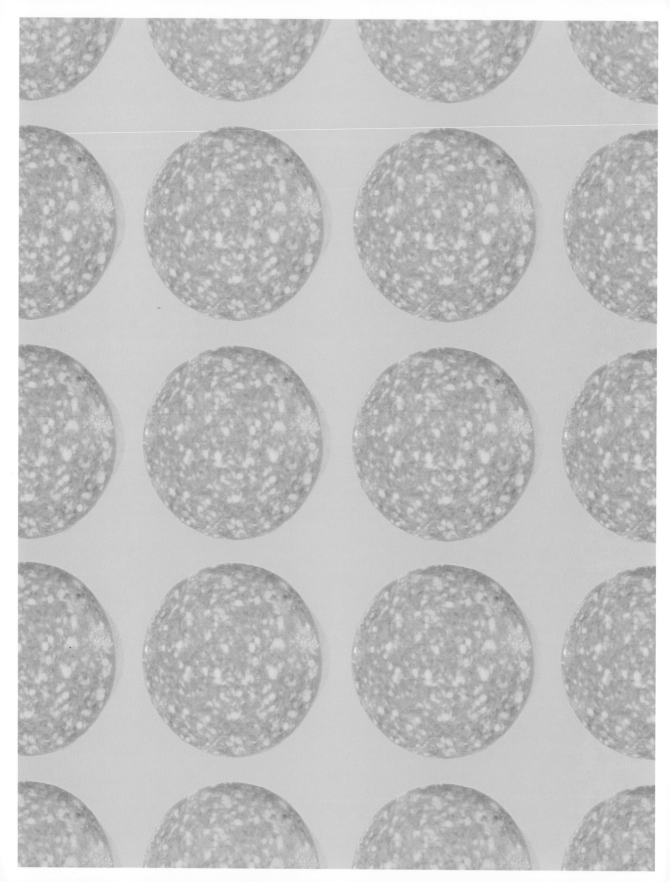

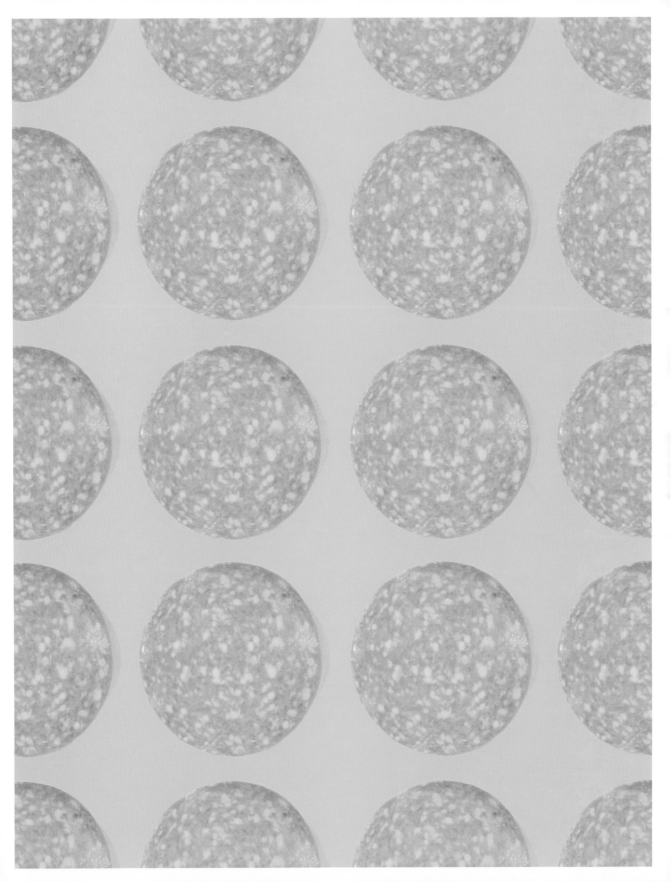

# WEEKNIGHT RAGU

## SERVES 4–6

*Spaghetti dinners were so insanely common growing up. It was an easy meal for my parents to throw together. I'm sure it was just jarred sauce and some minced beef but it was always a favourite, served with Wonder bread and butter or that pre-made garlic bread. That pre-made stuff was always too salty but I ate it anyways, because, garlic bread...*

450 g (1 lb) hot Italian sausage

1 tablespoon olive oil

2 × 400 g (1 × 28 oz) tins chopped tomatoes

½ medium onion, very roughly chopped into quarters

4 garlic cloves, smashed

15 g (½ cup) chopped parsley

¼ teaspoon freshly ground black pepper

½ teaspoon sea salt (or coarse kosher salt)

240 ml (1 cup) red wine or beef stock

450 g (1 lb) pasta (any will do)

Parmesan cheese, to serve

In a medium-sized pan break up and brown the sausage with the olive oil.

While that's happening, make the tomato sauce by blitzing the tomatoes, onion, garlic, parsley, salt, and pepper in a blender until smooth.

Once the meat has browned and the fat's rendered, forming brown bits on the bottom of the pan, deglaze it pan by adding the wine or beef stock and scraping the bits up. Cook for a couple of minutes until almost all the liquid has evaporated. Add the tomato sauce and simmer for 30 minutes.

Meanwhile bring a pot of water to a boil and cook your pasta according to the packet instructions.

When the pasta's done, toss with the sauce and serve with a load of Parmesan cheese.

# GARLIC BREAD

## MAKES 1 LOAF

*This is my current situation when it comes to garlic bread. Always served with spaghetti or the ragu, and it comes together while you make the pasta dish. It has that great classic flavour without sending you into a salt coma.*

125 g (½ cup) unsalted butter

8 garlic cloves, minced

sea salt and freshly ground black pepper

450 g (1 lb) loaf French bread

Preheat your oven to 180°C (350°F/Gas 4).

To make the garlic butter mixture, melt down the butter in a small saucepan over a low heat, add the garlic with a nice pinch of salt and pepper, and let it steep for about 20 minutes. Once it's had some time to hang out, split the loaf of French bread down the middle, brush on the garlic goodness and bake on a baking sheet lined with baking parchment, garlic-side up, for around 10–15 minutes, until golden brown.

# HONEY SRIRACHA CHICKEN SKEWERS

## SERVES 4–6

*Chicken skewers say 'summertime' in my book. I like to try and grill at least a couple of times a week during the summer when it doesn't get dark until, like, 9 – it's nice and warm, and you get to eat outside. If it's not tacos or burgers, it's probably something on a skewer. These are great because they hit all the tangy, sweet, and spicy notes and they come together super quick. What's even greater is that the chicken is also perfect for a little spin on taco nights.*

680 g (1½ lb) boneless, skinless chicken thighs, cut into 5 cm (2 in) pieces

½ teaspoon sea salt (or coarse kosher salt)

¼ teaspoon freshly ground black pepper

175 g (½ cup) honey

120 ml (½ cup) rice wine vinegar

3 tablespoons Sriracha

1 tablespoon toasted sesame seeds (optional)

Add the chicken to a large zip-top bag. In a bowl whisk together everything else besides the sesame seeds. Add 60 ml (¼ cup) of that to the chicken, shake and set aside. Put the rest of the sauce in a medium-sized saucepan, bring to a boil and cook for 2–3 minutes, until it has thickened slightly.

Remove the chicken from the bag and put on to skewers of your choice. I like a good flat metal skewer but bamboo works too (just remember you need to soak them for at least an hour beforehand so nobody goes up in flames).

After you skewer the chicken, heat up the BBQ grill to a medium–high heat. If you don't have a BBQ grill go ahead and use a griddle or some sort of flat cooking surface, also on medium–high heat.

Place skewers on the grill and brush with sauce, grill for 3–5 minutes, then turn and brush with sauce frequently until the meat is cooked through, another 5 minutes or so. Take off the grill and sprinkle with the sesame seeds, if using. Let the chicken rest for a few minutes before serving.

# HONEY SRIRACHA BRUSSELS SPROUTS

## SERVES 3–4

*That honey Sriracha combo from those skewers on the previous page is making another appearance. These sprouts are given the sweet and spicy treatment and are perfect for cool winter months, coming together in the oven quickly. And just like the chicken skewers, these also make a surprisingly good taco addition if you're feeling adventurous and vegetarian.*

1 tablespoon olive oil

2 tablespoons honey

1 tablespoon Sriracha

½ teaspoon sea salt (or coarse kosher salt)

pinch of black pepper

450 g (1 lb) Brussels sprouts, halved lengthwise

1 tablespoon toasted sesame seeds (optional)

Preheat the oven to 220°C (425°F/Gas 7) and line a baking sheet with baking parchment.

Add the olive oil, honey, Sriracha, and salt to a large bowl and toss the sprouts until they are evenly coated. Turn them all out onto the baking sheet so they're laying cut-side down and roast for 12–14 minutes, tossing halfway through, until brown and slightly crisp. Plate on to a serving dish and top with sesame seeds, if using.

# THE WHOLE ENCHILADA

## SERVES 6

*This enchilada sauce is one of those recipes I've had with me forever. I started making it when I first moved out on my own and have basically perfected it into what's here in the book. Its evolved from chilli powder to a more fresh-tasting dried chilli situation. The flavour's way deeper than the stuff you get in the tin, and sometimes I make it just to have as an addition to nachos (hold the applause), burritos, or steak fries. You can substitute the chicken for beef, beans, or squash. In fact, once you have this dish mastered you can take any path you want, tossing whatever you want in there, spreading your wings and flying to Enchiladatown.*

### For the sauce

960 ml (4 cups) low-sodium chicken stock

30 g (1 oz) dried guajillo chillies, stems and seeds removed*

175 g (6 oz) can of tomato paste

2 tablespoons plain (all-purpose) flour

2 tablespoons vegetable oil

½ teaspoon ground cumin

½ teaspoon ground coriander

2–3 teaspoons salt, depending on how low-sodium your chicken stock is

### For the assembly

16 corn tortillas, 10–13 cm (4–5 in) in diameter**

1 rotisserie chicken, shredded

20 g (⅓ cup) chopped fresh coriander (cilantro) plus more for garnish

1 shallot, minced

230 g (a scant 2 cups) grated Cheddar, or colby-jack cheese, divided

### For the bonus rice

1 teaspoon vegetable oil

200 g (1 cup) long-grain white rice

240 ml (1 cup) low-sodium chicken stock

* You can also look for ground chillies, usually sold near the dried chillies, but not chilli powder that has additional spices. This is actually my preferred ingredient for this sauce but it's a little more difficult to find. If you do find it, use 30 g (1 oz) and skip the step where the peppers steep.

** For the corn tortillas, this size restriction makes sure they can all fit in a 23 × 33 cm (9 × 13 in) pan. If you want to use larger tortillas then go ahead and use two 23 × 23 cm (9 × 9 in) baking dishes.

To make the sauce, bring the stock and chillies to a boil in a medium saucepan. Turn off the heat, cover and let them sit for 20 minutes, stirring halfway through to make sure they're all soaking in the tub. This is a good time to prepare the rest of the ingredients for the enchiladas. Once the 20 minutes are up, blitz in a blender for about 30 seconds, until smooth. It's okay if there are still some chilli flakes. Leave this in the blender for now.

Preheat your oven to 180°C (350°F/Gas 4). In the same saucepan you used for the chillies (no need to wash it out), combine the tomato paste, flour, oil, cumin, and coriander. Cook over a medium heat for about a minute, just until it all turns a darker shade of red. Add the blended chilli stock mixture and whisk to combine. Bring to a simmer and cook for 5 minutes, until the sauce has thickened slightly. Season to taste with the salt, then reserve a cup for the rice.

Prepare the corn tortillas by either heating them up directly over a high flame or in a dry frying pan, a minute or so on each side.

To assemble, start with the filling. Mix together the shredded chicken, coriander, shallot, half the cheese, and a soup ladle (or cup) of the enchilada sauce. Pour about half a ladle (½ cup) of enchilada sauce in the bottom of a 23 × 33 cm (9 × 13 in) pan. Place a good dollop of filling in each tortilla. Roll the tortillas and place seam-side down in the pan. Continue until the pan is full. There should be 2 rows in there – it might be a tight fit but it's cool. If you have any, leftover filling can be used in nachos or some sort of rice-bowl situation.

Pour the remaining enchilada sauce evenly over the top of the enchiladas. Top with the leftover cheese and bake for about 15 minutes, until the sauce is bubbling and the cheese has melted. Top with a sprinkling of fresh coriander and serve.

While the enchiladas bubble in the oven you can make the rice. In a medium saucepan with a tight-fitting lid, heat up the oil over a medium–high heat. Add the rice and cook until golden and toasty. Add the chicken stock and that reserved cup of enchilada sauce you took out of the batch earlier and bring the mixture to a boil. Reduce to a low simmer, cover, and cook for 17–20 minutes, until all the liquid has evaporated. Fluff with a fork and serve with the enchiladas.

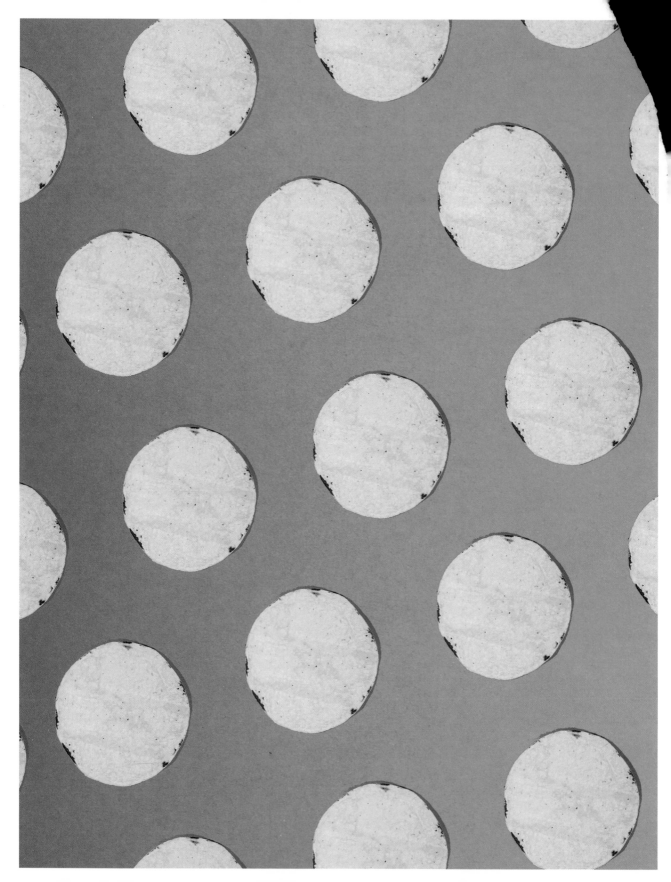

# TACOS, TACOS, TACOS

I actually had all these recipes within the Savoury chapter but quickly realised I'm all about that taco chapter life. I probably have tacos at least a couple of times a week – more during the summer when it makes a little more sense to grill. The tacos in here are just a little taste for Taco Tuesday, but feel free to mix up the meats and sauces, and top with anything you want. Also, elephant in the chapter: no homemade corn tortillas. I'm not a fan of the consistency or flavour, and it's kind of way easier to respectfully warm up a really good shop-bought one.

# TACO TOPPERS

Friends don't let friends eat plain tacos. I've got a few ideas in the chapter with salsas and tangy pickled onions, but there's a few other options:

1. The cheese: I like cotija on just about everything but I like it the most on just about every taco. It's a hard salty cheese, similar to Parmesan, but perfect for all tacos. If you can't find cotija look for queso fresco or just try any other Mexican cheese you can get your hands on until you find one you really like. Feta can work, too.

2. The crunch factor: I've pickled radishes here (page 80) that give a nice crunch and a slight tangy flavour, but an alternative if you didn't want the tang is a small white onion really finely minced. It's going to give some flavour and texture difference, just like the radishes.

3. The fresh factor: this for me is almost always in the form of coriander (cilantro) but I also use any of the salsas in the chapter as well as lime wedges, which add a nice bright zing.

~~~~~~~~~~~~~~~~~~~~~~~~~~~~~

# PICKLED RADISH

## MAKES ABOUT 375 G (1½ CUPS)

~~~~~~~~~~~~~~~~~~~~~~~~~~~~~

*One of my favourite taco toppers is the hot pink quick-pickled radish. It adds a crunch and a slight zing to the tacos, plus that colour is enough to make anyone go crazy.*

10 radishes

juice of 1 lime

½ teaspoon sea salt (or coarse
    kosher salt)

To prepare the radishes, trim the ends off and cut them into medium-sized slices. Turn over the radish so it's lying flat and slice again to create matchsticks.

Add these to an airtight container that holds 250 g (2 cups), then add the lime juice and salt, and shake to combine. These are ready to go right away, but if you want that crazy bright pink colour, let them marinate in the fridge for 2–3 hours.

They will keep in the fridge for 3 days in an airtight container.

# AVOCADO SALSA

## MAKES ABOUT 500 ML (2 CUPS)

*This stuff is the golden show pony of the taco chapter. A lot of taquerias/taco trucks around Southern California serve this along with all the other topping options, which is how I became addicted. It's so, so simple to make and tastes really great on pretty much everything; get ready to be amazed.*

1 large avocado, roughly chopped

3 tablespoons minced shallot

2 tablespoons lime juice (from 1 lime)

1 teaspoon sea salt (or coarse kosher salt)

1 jalapeño, stemmed (remove half the seeds if you don't want it as spicy)

300 ml (1¼ cups) water

30 g (1 cup) coriander (cilantro)

Combine all the ingredients in a blender and blitz for about 30 seconds, until smooth. Refrigerate for at least an hour to let all the flavours come together.

This will keep in the fridge for 3 days in an airtight container, but I seriously doubt you'll have any left.

~~~~~~~~~~~~~~~~~~~~~~~~~~~

# SALSA VERDE

## MAKES 750 ML (3 CUPS)

~~~~~~~~~~~~~~~~~~~~~~~~~~~

*One taco topper that everyone should definitely make is the tomatillo-based Salsa Verde. It's just a handful of ingredients that get blended together and it elevates any taco/rice bowl/nacho situation it comes in contact with. If you can't get your hands on tomatillos, you can substitute them with underripe tomatoes and a squeeze of lime juice.*

450 g (1 lb) tomatillos

2 garlic cloves, smashed

1 jalapeño, roughly chopped, seeds
    removed for a mild salsa, or keep them
    if you like it spicy

1 teaspoon sea salt (or coarse kosher salt)

350 ml (1½ cups) water

2 spring onions (scallions), thinly sliced

25 g (½ cup) coriander (cilantro),
    roughly chopped

juice of ½ lime

To prep the tomatillos, peel off the husk and rinse them under cold water. Once clean, cut them in half and add to a medium-sized saucepan with the garlic, jalapeño, salt, and water. Don't worry if they're not fully submerged. Bring to a simmer and cook for 10 minutes, stirring occasionally to make sure all the tomatillos are saying hey to the water. Set aside to cool.

Remove the tomatillos from the water, then add them and the rest of the ingredients to a blender and blitz until smooth, around 15–20 seconds. Because the ingredients are really hot, don't put the full lid back on the blender when you do this, as it could lead to an explosion. If your blender has a centre lid which can come out, remove it. If not, just use a tea towel. Pour into a container and cool to room temperature before placing in the fridge. Chill for a couple of hours so the flavours to infuse and get familiar with each other.

This will keep in the fridge for up to 1 week in an airtight container.

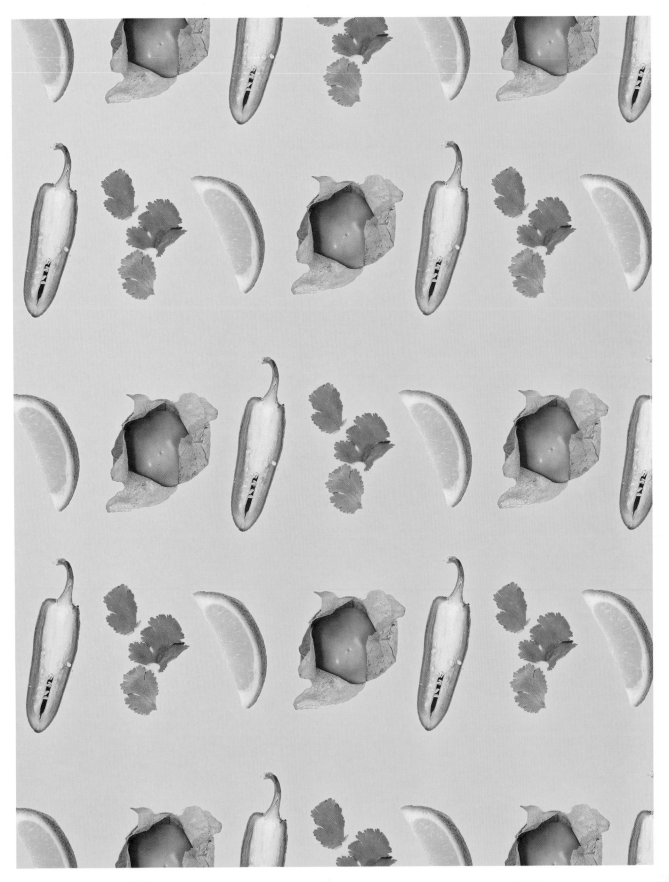

# RESTAURANT SALSA

## MAKES 750 ML (3 CUPS)

*Secretly everyone's favourite part of going out to a Mexican restaurant is gorging yourself on chips and salsa so you don't have room for the actual food you just ordered. Well now you can do that at home!*

450 g (1 lb) ripe tomatoes

1 jalapeño, halved and seeded

5–6 green onions, depending on size,
    roots trimmed

2 cloves garlic

1 teaspoon sea salt (or coarse kosher salt)

1 teaspoon freshly ground black pepper

juice of ½ lime

15 g (½ cup) coriander (cilantro)

170 ml (¾ cup) water

Turn on your grill to high and line a baking sheet with aluminium foil.

Cut the tomatoes in half and place cut-side down on the prepared baking sheet with the jalapeño and green onions. Grill on high for 10 minutes, making sure you open all the windows and turn on a fan so you don't set off the fire alarm.

After 10 minutes remove the vegetables from under the grill. They're going to look burned to crap and you're gonna panic that your salsa's ruined, but they're supposed to be like that – calm down!

Let vegetables cool down for about 30 minutes, then add them all to a blender (all of it, even the crispy black parts of the green onions) with everything else. Blend for about 20 seconds, until fairly smooth, then transfer to a container to chill in the fridge. In a couple of hours it'll be ready to inhale.

This will keep in the fridge for up to 1 week in an airtight container.

# CARNE ASADA TACOS

## SERVES 4–6

*I think carne asada is one of those things that's always over-complicated with crazy marinades and voodoo magic to try and get what happens in a taqueria, but the truth is that's not necessary. All you need is a good hunk of meat, some Steak Seasoning, and maybe a hit of lime if you're feeling glamorous. Less is more in this case – and that's coming from a guy who'd glue rhinestones to his face if his skin wasn't so sensitive. I love a good carne asada on just about everything but the best way to me is in 1–7 tacos.*

675 g (1½ lb) skirt or flank steak

2 teaspoons Steak Seasoning (page 194), or a teaspoon each of sea salt and freshly ground black pepper

1 packet of corn tortillas

*To serve*

fresh lime juice (optional)

Avocado Salsa (page 82)

handful of coriander (cilantro), roughly chopped

1 white onion, diced

cotija cheese (use feta if you can't find this)

Preheat the pan or grill over a high heat and season both sides of the meat. Lay the meat in the pan or on the grill and leave it undisturbed for 4 minutes, flip and leave for another 4 minutes. If your frying pan is too small to fit the meat, just cut it in half (you won't need to do this on the BBQ). Depending on your thickness of meat, this usually yields a little bit of a medium cook. If you like your meat super well done, then go for a couple more minutes after you flip it. Let the meat rest for 15 minutes before slicing into strips, against the grain.

Prepare the corn tortillas by either heating them up directly over a high flame or in a dry frying pan, a minute or so on each side. Serve with a squeeze of lime juice (if using), Avocado Salsa, coriander, onion, and cotija, or any of the taco toppers you wanna try.

~~~~~~~~~~~~~~~~~~~~~~~~~~~~~~~~~~~~~~~~~

# BREAKFAST TACOS

## SERVES 2

~~~~~~~~~~~~~~~~~~~~~~~~~~~~~~~~~~~~~~~~~

*I know this is a breakfast dish and it's not in the Breakfast chapter but this is Tacos, Tacos, Tacos so I reckon it should be here. This is one of those breakfasts that's perfect when you're super hungry but way too lazy or hungover to handle too much time in the kitchen. Just a little bit of scrambled eggs with my foolproof method and breakfast is ready in, like, 10 minutes. Maybe 45 if you're trying it with only one eye open. If you're feeling extra good about it all, fry up some chorizo until it's nice and crispy in the pan before you add the eggs.*

1 teaspoon vegetable oil

4 large eggs, beaten

1 packet of corn tortillas

*To serve*

Restaurant Salsa (page 87)

cotija cheese (use feta if you can't find this)

Turn the heat up to high and let a nonstick pan get nice and hot. Add the oil then grab a rubber spatula and add the eggs to the hot pan. Immediately start moving the eggs around, scraping the bottom of the pan, working quickly so nobody burns. The goal is to be quick about it and move the eggs around until they're just cooked. This literally takes a minute, maybe 2. Set aside once they're cooked.

Prepare the corn tortillas by either heating them up directly over a high flame or in a dry frying pan, a minute or so on each side. Make the tacos by placing some egg on a tortilla then topping with Restaurant Salsa and cotija cheese, or whatever toppings you fancy.

# CORN AND CHICKPEA TACOS

## SERVES 4

*Sometimes tacos just happen. Sometimes you don't want to get our of your pyjamas to leave your apartment so you use the frozen corn and tinned chickpeas you have to make dinner and never look back. Bonus points that it's accidentally vegetarian and perfect for when those friends come over for Taco Tuesday.*

350 g (1½ cups) fresh or frozen sweetcorn

400 g (14½ oz) tin chickpeas

1 tablespoon olive oil

3 spring onions (scallions), thinly sliced

3 tablespoons Taco Seasoning (page 197)

80 ml (⅓ cup) water

1 packet of corn tortillas

*To serve*

Pickled Radish (page 80)

1 avocado, sliced

handful of coriander (cilantro),
    roughly chopped

cotija cheese (use feta if you can't
    find this)

If you're using the frozen corn, thaw it out first by putting it in a colander and running it under cold water. Once it's ready, drain the chickpeas and rinse them too.

Heat the olive oil over a medium–high heat in a large frying pan and add the corn, chickpeas, and spring onions. Cook for 3–5 minutes until the spring onions soften and the corn and chickpeas start to brown.

Add the Taco Seasoning and water, then stir to mix and cook for about 5 minutes, or until almost all the liquid has evaporated.

Prepare the corn tortillas by either heating them up directly over a high flame or in a dry frying pan, a minute or so on each side.

To serve, add the corn and chickpea mixture to a warmed tortilla. Top with Pickled Radish, avocado slices, fresh coriander and cotija cheese.

# CHICKEN TINGA TACOS

## SERVES 4–6

*This is definitely one of my favourites in the book. It's incredibly simple with little hands-on time and huge results. It's smokey from the chipotle, a little spicy, and a little sweet. It'll impress all your friends and it costs next to nothing to whip up – it's like the queen of affordable dinners. If this is something you want to set and forget then you're in luck, because there's that option below.*

900 g (2 lb) boneless, skinless chicken thighs, seasoned with sea salt and freshly ground black pepper

2 × 400 g (1 × 28 oz) tins chopped tomatoes

25 g (½ cup) coriander (cilantro), roughly chopped

4 garlic cloves, smashed and peeled

½ medium onion, quartered

½ teaspoon sea salt (or coarse kosher salt)

½ teaspoon freshly ground black pepper

2 tablespoons chipotle purée or paste

1 bay leaf

1 packet of corn tortillas

*To serve*

Pickled Radish (page 80)

handful of coriander (cilantro), roughly chopped

cotija cheese (use feta if you can't find this)

Preheat your oven to 180°C (350°F/Gas 4).

In a large heavy pan lightly brown the chicken thighs on both sides in 2 batches.

While they brown, make the sauce by blitzing everything else except the bay leaf and corn tortillas in a blender until smooth.

Once the chicken is browned, remove from the pan and set aside. Using the same pan, pour in the sauce, scraping the bottom of the pan to loosen any chicken bits that may have caught. Add the chicken and the bay leaf to the sauce, carefully mixing to combine. Gently simmer for 30 minutes, covered, then remove the lid and cook for an additional 30 minutes, until the sauce has thickened and the chicken shreds easily.

If you're feeling your slow-cook: brown the chicken, place in a slow cooker, mix in the sauce and bay leaf and cook on high for 4–6 hours, or low for 6–8 hours.

Prepare the corn tortillas by either heating them up directly over a high flame or in a dry frying pan, a minute or so on each side.

To serve, remove the bay leaf from the sauce. Add the chicken mixture to a warmed tortilla, top with Pickled Radish, coriander, and cotija cheese.

# ROASTED CHIPOTLE PRAWN TACOS

## SERVES 4

*If seafood tacos are more your thing then you can have a dozen of these. They come together super-fast in the oven. Super-fast enough that dinner might actually take less than 20 minutes. Model is shown wearing Avocado Salsa (page 82), coriander, and cotija cheese. Yes, that's cheese on top; whoever said no cheese on seafood can take one of these to the face.*

450 g (1 lb) prawns (shrimps), peeled and
   deveined
2 tablespoons olive oil
2 tablespoons chipotle purée or paste
juice of 1 lime
sea salt and freshly ground black pepper
1 packet of corn tortillas

To serve
Avocado Salsa (page 82)
handful of coriander (cilantro),
   roughly chopped
cotija cheese (use feta if you can't
   find this)

Preheat your oven to 200°C (400°F/Gas 6).

Line a large baking tray with baking parchment and toss the prawns with the oil, chipotle purée, lime juice, salt, and pepper. Please go wash your hands now because I don't want you to burn any parts of your body with the chipotle sauce that is all over your hands.

Roast for 5–7 minutes, just until you can see them turn pink and curl slightly; don't overcook them or they'll go rubbery. Let the prawns rest for just a couple of minutes before serving.

Prepare the corn tortillas by either heating them up directly over a high flame or in a dry frying pan, a minute or so on each side.

To serve, spread the prawns on top of a warm tortilla. Top with Avocado Salsa, coriander and cotija cheese.

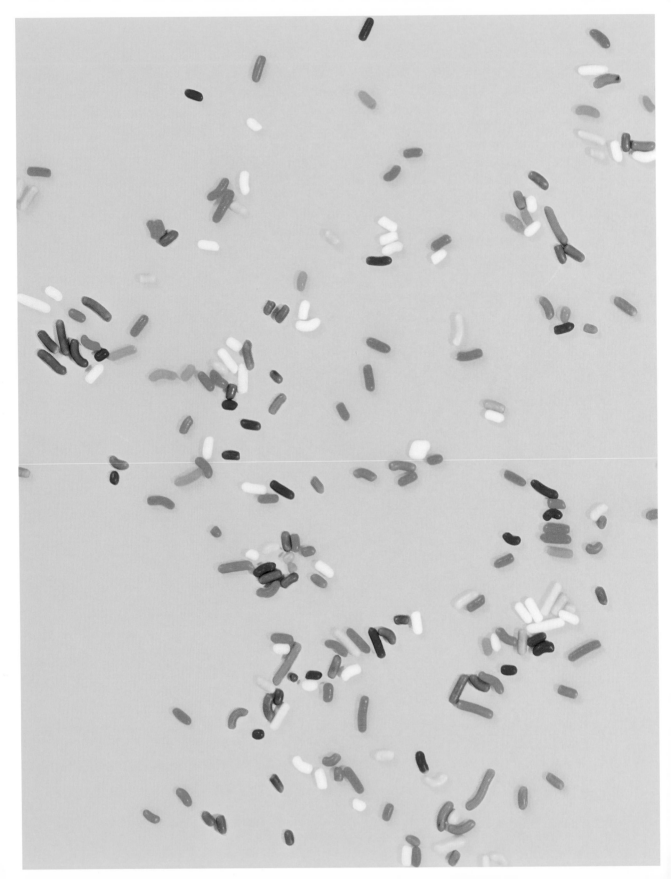

SWEETS

All the sweets, for any occasion. I love a good, simple dessert that's comforting and impressive at the same time and all of these recipes fit that bill. There's almost always a dessert emergency and I have you covered – from surprise birthdays to surprise guests, to surprise I-need-dessert-in-my-mouth-right-now.

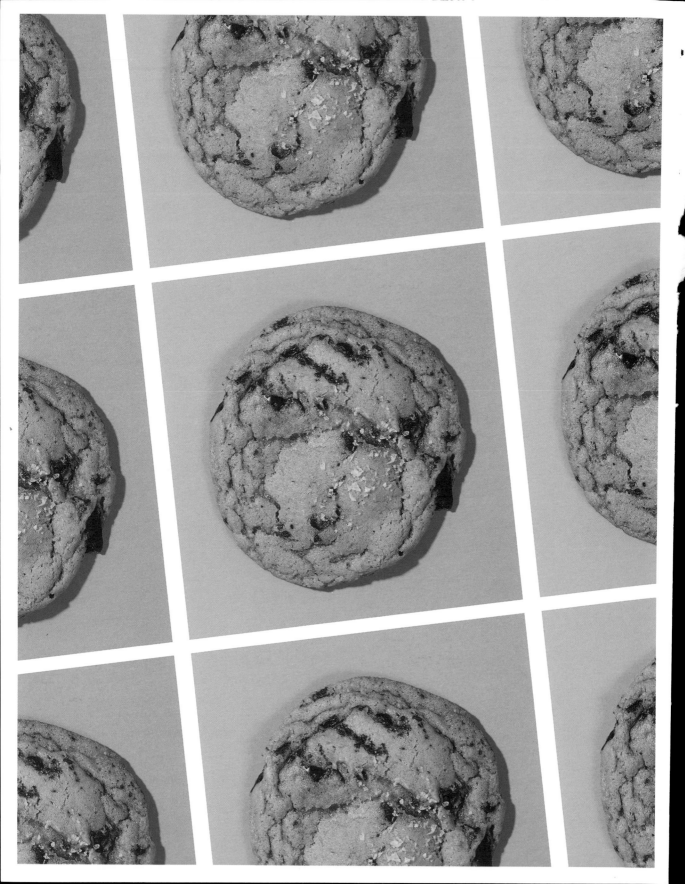

~~~~~~~~~~~~~~~~~~~~~~

# DARK CHOCOLATE CHUNK COOKIES WITH SEA SALT

## MAKES ABOUT 3 DOZEN

~~~~~~~~~~~~~~~~~~~~~~

*I know the world doesn't need another chocolate chip cookie recipe but I figured it's my book so I'm allowed to do what I want. This cookie's got a perfectly gooey, chewy centre, flaky sea salt, and my patented chocolate confetti technique to make sure you get a taste of chocolate with every bite.*

300 g (2 cups) dark chocolate chunks
    or chips (or just be yourself and use
    300 g/2 cups of whatever chips)

375 g (3 cups) plain (all-purpose) flour

1½ teaspoons baking powder

1 teaspoon bicarbonate of soda
    (baking soda)

1 teaspoon flaky sea salt, plus extra
    to sprinkle

220 g (1 cup) unsalted butter, cubed

300 g (1½ cups) light brown sugar

115 g (½ cup) white granulated sugar

2 large eggs

1 tablespoon pure vanilla extract

Preheat your oven to 180°C (350°F/Gas 4).

If you didn't chop your chocolate from a bar, give the pieces a few chops to break it up to make the confetti.

In a large bowl, whisk together the flour, baking powder, bicarbonate of soda, and salt. Set aside. In a medium-sized saucepan, melt half the butter completely. Turn off the heat and add the remaining butter, letting the residual heat melt this. Once it's melted, use a rubber spatula or wooden spoon to stir in the sugars.

Add the eggs one at a time, blending completely after each one, then add the vanilla extract. Pour the wet ingredients into the flour mixture and fold just until there's barely any trace of flour. Add the chocolate chips and stir until just combined and the chocolate chips are evenly dispersed. Cover with cling film (plastic wrap) and refrigerate for at least 1 hour, preferably 4. The flavours meld a little better this way.

Scoop the dough out on a baking sheet using a medium-sized cookie scoop, or about 1½ tablespoons of dough, and sprinkle with sea salt. I like to bake 9 on a sheet. Bake for 12–14 minutes on baking parchment, one baking sheet at a time, rotating the sheet halfway through. You want them to be slightly golden brown around the edges and appear to be under-baked. This ensures beautifully chewy cookies. Cool for 5 minutes on the baking sheet then transfer to a cooling rack.

# CHOCOLATE ESPRESSO SNICKERDOODLES

## MAKES ABOUT 3 DOZEN

*Sometimes you just need to remix a classic. I love a good snickerdoodle just as much as the next person, but sometimes I want chocolate with my cinnamon and maybe a good shot of espresso. The 3 go so well together – a polygamist match made in heaven. It's a gooey, chewy, cinnamon and chocolate explosion with that hint of espresso that goes really well with a glass of milk, or as a building block for a killer ice cream sandwich (see picture overleaf).*

280 g (2¼ cups) plain (all-purpose) flour

80 g (⅔ cup) unsweetened cocoa powder

1½ teaspoons cream of tartar

1 teaspoon bicarbonate of soda
   (baking soda)

½ teaspoon sea salt (or coarse kosher salt)

226 g (1 cup) butter, softened

2 teaspoons espresso instant coffee
   (powder)

200 g (1 cup) light brown sugar

170 g (¾ cup) white granulated sugar

2 large eggs

2 teaspoons pure vanilla extract

2 teaspoons cinnamon

3 tablespoons cane sugar*

* This makes the cookies sparkle more, which is always a good thing. If you can't find it, go ahead and use regular white granulated sugar.

Sift together the flour, cocoa, cream of tartar, bicarbonate of soda, and salt in a medium-sized bowl.

In another bowl, use an electric mixer to cream the butter, coffee, brown sugar, and white granulated sugar until light and fluffy, about 2 minutes.

Add the eggs one at a time, making sure the first one is completely blended before adding the second one with the vanilla extract. Then add the cocoa-flour mixture in 2 batches so it doesn't fly everywhere, mixing just until combined. Refrigerate the dough for at least an hour to firm up.

Preheat your oven to 180°C (350°F/Gas 3) and line a baking sheet with baking parchment.

Combine the cinnamon and sugar in a small bowl or pie dish, then use a medium cookie scoop (or 1½ tablespoons) to portion out dough and roll in cinnamon sugar to coat. Place on the baking sheet 5 cm (2 in) apart and bake for 8–10 minutes until slightly flattened and crackly. You want them to be a little underbaked to ensure maximum chew. Cool for 5 minutes on the baking sheet, then transfer to a cooling rack to cool completely.

# NUTELLA BROWNIE TART

## SERVES AT LEAST 6

*Welcome to my brownie offering. This bad boy is super fudgy, comes together in one saucepan, and looks extra fancy because we're cooking it in a tart tin (nail-painting emoji to the max). If the round tart tin isn't your thing then go ahead and cook the brownies in a parchment-paper-lined 20 × 20 cm (8 × 8 in) baking sheet for 5 minutes longer.*

125 g (½ cup) unsalted butter

155 g (½ cup) Nutella

100 g (3½ oz) good-quality dark (bittersweet) chocolate, chopped

80 g (⅓ cup) white granulated sugar

¼ teaspoon sea salt (or coarse kosher salt)

1 teaspoon pure vanilla extract

2 large eggs

60 g (½ cup) plain (all-purpose) flour

icing (confectioners') sugar, to serve (optional)

Preheat your oven to 180°C (350°F/Gas 4) and grease a 25 cm (10 in) loose-bottomed tart tin.

In a medium saucepan, melt down the butter and Nutella. Remove from the hob and add the chocolate, letting it sit for a minute or so to melt from the residual heat. Then whisk it all together to make a beautiful, glossy mess that you probably want to bathe in.

Add in the sugar, salt, and vanilla extract and whisk to combine. Add the eggs one at a time, fully incorporating the first before adding the second. Carefully add the flour and mix just until the flour disappears.

Pour the mixture into the prepared tart tin and bake for 25–30 minutes, until the top is nice and glossy and sort of crackled. It won't look 100 per cent done when you take it out but that means not having a dry hockey puck.

Cool completely before serving to ensure the best texture. If you want to eat it warm, maybe with vanilla ice cream, let it cool completely after baking, then pop it in the oven for 5 minutes at 180°C (350°F/Gas 4) before serving. Dust with icing sugar before serving, if you like.

# VANILLA APPLE CRUMBLE

## SERVES 4–6

*This is winter in a dessert, at it's finest. Warm spiced filling with a crumbly vanilla-punched topping. I might actually prefer a crumble to a pie; I love the extra flavours and texture you get from the crumble, plus it takes way less time and finesse, which is something my hands lack when it comes to pretty pie crusts. If you don't vibe with apples, feel free to use pears or even peaches if they're in season.*

*For the topping*

125 g (½ cup) unsalted butter

1 vanilla pod, split, seeds scraped and
    reserved

125 g (1 cup) plain (all-purpose) flour

70 g (⅓ cup) light brown sugar

¼ teaspoon sea salt (or coarse kosher salt)

60 g (½ cup) roughly chopped walnuts

*For the filling*

50 g (¼ cup) light brown sugar

1 tablespoon plain (all-purpose) flour

1 teaspoon cinnamon

½ teaspoon nutmeg

¼ teaspoon sea salt (coarse kosher salt)

4 large apples, thinly sliced (I particularly
    like Fuji or gala for this)

Preheat your oven to 190°C (375°F/Gas 5) and grease a 20 cm (8 in) square baking dish.

In a small saucepan, melt the butter. Add the vanilla pod and the seeds to the melted butter and let it steep for 20 minutes while you prepare the rest of the ingredients.

To make the filling, combine the brown sugar, flour, cinnamon, nutmeg, and salt. Toss with the apples and set aside.

For the topping, mix together the flour, brown sugar, salt, and walnuts. Pour in the melted vanilla butter and mix it around until everything is coated.

Add the filling mixture to the prepared dish, then evenly distribute crumble over the top.

Bake for 30–40 minutes, until the top is golden brown and the filling is bubbly. Serve with the biggest scoop of vanilla ice cream you can fit on your plate.

# BROWN BUTTER & WALNUT BLONDIES

## MAKES 16

*Do blondies have more fun? I might have to say yes (hairflip). For those of you that don't know, blondies are the chocolate-free cousin of the brownie. There's a deep toffee flavour from the brown sugar and all the walnuts in the world that just send these over the top for me. Yes, of course you can add chocolate to these but then it's bordering on chocolate-chip-cookie territory and I already have a recipe for those in the book – plus that toffee flavour needs his spotlight.*

90 g (6 tablespoons) unsalted butter, cubed

200 g (1 cup) light brown sugar

1 large egg

1 teaspoon pure vanilla extract

125 g (1 cup) plain (all-purpose) flour

½ teaspoon baking powder

½ teaspoon sea salt (or coarse kosher salt)

125 g (1 cup) coarsely chopped walnuts

In a medium-sized saucepan melt down the butter and continue to cook until the fizzling stops and the butter turns a light amber colour (don't do this in any pan with a coating or else you won't be able to see the colour and will probably burn the butter). Remove the pan from the heat and let cool for about 15 minutes. You can preheat your oven to 180°C (350°F/Gas 4), dance, and grease and line a 20 × 20 cm (8 × 8 in) cake tin with baking parchment while you're waiting.

After the butter's cooled down, stir in the brown sugar, then stir in the egg and vanilla extract until it's nice and combined. Sprinkle the flour, baking powder, and salt into the batter and stir until just combined.

Fold in the walnuts, then smooth the batter into the prepared cake tin and bake for 20–25 minutes, until lightly browned and the top is all crinkly. DO NOT OVERBAKE. Let them cool completely in the tin before removing and serving.

# MY GRANDMA'S BLACKBERRY COBBLER

## SERVES 4–5

*As soon as the realisation hit that a cookbook was happening I called my grandma and asked for her cobbler recipe. Growing up we'd visit my grandparents during the summer and pick a ton of berries and my grandma would make it for us. It's a serious food memory and I love it. The topping is almost like a cake, but it's SO. FREAKING. GOOD. If you ever have a load of blackberries and want to feel your face explode from happiness, then make this cobbler.*

### For the filling

680 g (24 oz) fresh or thawed frozen
    blackberries (or whatever fruit you feel
    like really, about 680 g/6 cups)

1½ tablespoons cornflour (cornstarch)

⅓ cup white granulated sugar

pinch of salt

### For the topping

90 g (¾ cups) plain (all-purpose) flour

2 tablespoons white granulated sugar

2 teaspoons baking powder

¼ teaspoon sea salt (or coarse kosher salt)

120 ml (½ cup) whole (full-fat) milk

60 ml (¼ cup) vegetable oil

1 large egg

1 batch Vanilla Buttermilk Ice Cream
    (page 147), to serve

Preheat your oven to 180°C (350°F/Gas 4).

In a 20 × 20 cm (8 × 8 in) cake tin, toss together the berries, cornflour, sugar, and salt.

In a medium-sized bowl, mix together the flour, sugar, baking powder, and salt.

Pour the milk into another medium-sized bowl, add the oil and the egg, and beat until it all comes together.

Add the wet ingredients to the dry and mix together, just until there's no flour left – a few lumps are okay.

Using a large spoon, distribute the topping over the filling in 5 sort-of blobs – one in each corner then one in the centre – and spread them out slightly. Don't worry if some of the filling is peeping through.

Bake in the preheated oven for 40–45 minutes, until lightly golden brown and a toothpick inserted into the topping comes out clean. Serve with the Vanilla Buttermilk Ice Cream.

# CELEBRATION CAKE

## SERVES 8–10

*When it comes to the moment where you're kicking down doors and singing Happy Birthday, this is the cake you should have in your hands. I don't know, I guess kicking down doors is optional but this is my favourite cake for celebrations. The cake itself is a riff off this magic egg- and dairy-free cake that's been around since the Depression era. I've tweaked it to have buttermilk because it makes it taste even better. It's so good, so simple, and there's no need to know how to decorate a cake! Win-win for those of us with hands that double as wrecking balls.*

### For the cake

280 g (2¼ cups) plain (all-purpose) flour

400 g (1¾ cups) white granulated sugar

1 teaspoon sea salt (or coarse kosher salt)

2 teaspoons bicarbonate of soda (baking soda)

125 g (1 cup) cocoa powder

2 tablespoons hot water

2 teaspoons espresso instant coffee (powder)

200 ml (¾ cup plus 2 tablespoons) water

240 ml (1 cup) buttermilk

160 ml (⅔ cup) vegetable or melted coconut oil

1 tablespoon pure vanilla extract

### For the filling and ganache *

225 g (8 oz) cream cheese, softened

230 g (1 cup) white granulated sugar

pinch of salt

1 teaspoon pure vanilla extract

240 ml (1 cup) double (heavy) cream, divided

175 g (6 oz) good-quality dark (bittersweet) chocolate, chopped

* If you just want a 23 x 33 cm (9 x 13 in) cake, bake all the batter in that size tin and double the filling and ganache. Spread the ganache over the top first, cool completely in the fridge, then top with the cream-cheese filling. No splitting or stacking necessary, and it's still very delicious.

Preheat your oven to 180°C (350°F/Gas 4) and grease 2 x 23 cm (9 in) cake tins. Trace and cut out 2 x 23 cm (9 in) baking parchment circles using the bottom of your cake tins, then place the parchment on the bottom of the tins and grease the parchment.

To make the cake, sift together the flour, sugar, salt, bicarbonate of soda, and cocoa powder in a large bowl.

In a second bowl or 1 litre (4 cup) measuring jug, add 2 tablespoons of hot water (either boiled or from the hot tap), then add the coffee, stirring to dissolve. Add the cold water, buttermilk, oil, and vanilla and mix together.

Add the wet ingredients to the dry ingredients and mix until it's just combined. Evenly distribute the batter between the 2 cake tins and bake for 35–40 minutes, or until a toothpick inserted in the centre comes out clean. When the cakes come out, let them cool for 30 minutes, then invert onto a wire rack to cool completely.

Now make the cream-cheese filling. Take the very soft cream cheese and sift in your white granulated sugar. Add the pinch of salt and beat with an electric mixer until light and fluffy. Add the vanilla extract and 80 ml (⅓ cup) of the double cream and beat on high until it's all come together in one big fluffy mass. Set in the fridge until ready to use.

When you're ready to assemble, place one layer onto a cake stand and cover with the cream-cheese -filling. Place the second layer top-down on top of that.

Make the dark chocolate ganache by warming up the remaining 160 ml (⅔ cup) cream on the stove, being careful not to boil it, then pouring it over the chocolate and letting it sit for a couple of minutes. Whisk together until smooth and glossy and add to the top of the cake, taking care with the spreading so it barely starts to drip over the edge. Refrigerate the cake until ready to serve, and try to make this cake in advance: it gets a little better if it sits in the fridge for the day.

# CARAMEL BANANA PUDDING

## SERVES 8

*Growing up, one of my favourite desserts at potluck gatherings was banana pudding – classic and pure, with box pudding mix, wafers, and at least one tub of cool whip. This is a little more 'advanced' than that, tossing out the box mix and cool whip but keeping the Nilla wafers. If you don't live in the US, try substituting the Nilla wafers with a crunchy, vanilla-flavoured biscuit such as Rich Tea or a Marie.*

140 g (⅔ cup) white granulated sugar

2 tablespoons water

960 ml (4 cups) whole (full-fat) milk

40 g (⅓ cup) cornflour (cornstarch)

¼ teaspoon sea salt (or coarse kosher salt)

1 teaspoon pure vanilla extract

1 pint double (heavy) cream

2 tablespoons white granulated sugar

4 large bananas

350 g (12 oz) box of Nilla wafers (see note above)

sliced almonds, to garnish

To make the pudding, add the sugar and water to a large saucepan. (You'll need a large pan as the milk foams up.) Cook over a medium heat without stirring (an occasional swirl is okay to ensure no burning) until the mixture turns almost an amber colour. A good trick is to stop as soon as you see wisps of smoke coming off. As soon as this happens, turn the heat off and carefully add 750 ml (3 cups) of the milk. The mixture will seize and bubble, and you're gonna think it's ruined, but just patiently whisk for a couple of minutes and it should all smooth out. Once the mixture is smooth, bring it to a simmer and cook for 5 minutes. Meanwhile stir together the remaining milk with the cornflour, salt, and vanilla. After the 5 minutes, whisk the milk and cornflour mixture into the caramel. Bring to a simmer and cook for 30 seconds. Transfer the pudding to a bowl, cover with cling film (plastic wrap), and refrigerate until completely cool.

Once the pudding is cool, whip the cream and sugar together to soft peaks, then set aside.

Now we assemble: peel and slice the bananas right beforehand so there's less time to brown. You can use either a large trifle dish or 8 small dishes or drinking glasses). Our goal is 3 layers, so start with ⅓ of the vanilla wafers for the foundation, then ⅓ of the bananas, then ⅓ of the pudding, then ⅓ of the whipped cream. Continue 2 more times so that you end up with the whipped cream on the top. Refrigerate for at least 30 minutes, and for no longer than 3 hours. Top with sliced almonds, and serve.

# RUM & RAISIN BREAD PUDDING
## WITH MAPLE WHIPPED CREAM
### SERVES 8–10

*This is one of those recipes where you know it's old. It's another recipe from my grandma, who got it from her mother, and the amount of each ingredient alone is enough to excite me. Don't be super alarmed at the amounts: it's not overboard, but it's perfect for a large gathering and can easily be halved and thrown in a 20 × 20 cm (8 × 8 in) dish.*

450 g (1 lb) loaf of French bread or brioche, roughly chopped into 4 cm (1½ in) cubes

60 ml (¼ cup) rum

85 g (⅔ cup) raisins

12 large eggs

285 g (1¼ cups) white granulated sugar

950 ml (1 quart) whole (full-fat) milk

1 tablespoon pure vanilla extract

1 teaspoon cinnamon

½ teaspoon sea salt (or kosher salt)

30 g (2 tablespoons) unsalted butter, diced

### For the maple whipped cream

240 ml (1 cup) double (heavy) cream

2 tablespoons pure maple syrup

Preheat your oven to 150°C (300°F/Gas 2) and line a large baking sheet with baking parchment.

Toast the bread cubes for 15–20 minutes until lightly golden brown and dried out. The dryer the bread, the better it will soak up the custard, so leave it for as long as you can. Gently warm up the rum in a small saucepan with the raisins, then turn off the heat and let it cool completely.

Turn the oven up to 180°C (350°F/Gas 4) and grease a 23 × 33 cm (9 × 13 in) baking dish.

In your largest bowl, whisk together the eggs and sugar to combine, then add the milk, vanilla, cinnamon, and salt. Whisk all that together then add the rum-raisin mixture and the bread cubes. Mix well then pour into the prepared dish. Lightly press down to make sure everyone gets a turn with the custard, then let sit for about 5 minutes.

Evenly distribute the butter over the top, then bake in the preheated oven for 45 minutes, until lightly golden brown.

To make the maple whipped cream, beat the cream and pure maple syrup together until soft peaks form. Serve with the warm bread pudding after it has rested for about 30 minutes out of the oven.

# RASPBERRY MARSHMALLOWS

## MAKES ABOUT 30

*Now just to be upfront, this is probably the most difficult recipe in the book, but please don't let that put you off! They're not necessarily hard to whip up, they just take a little confidence – and maybe a second person – but they're worth it. You can't just go out and buy raspberry marshmallows and sometimes your s'mores need a little oomph-on-oomph action.*

175 g (about 1½ cups) frozen raspberries, thawed*

2 tablespoons water

2 × 7 g (¼ oz) packets gelatine

230 g (1 cup) white granulated sugar

160 ml (⅔ cup) light corn syrup

¼ teaspoon sea salt (or coarse kosher salt)

1 tablespoon pure vanilla extract

*For the marshmallow coating*

1 tablespoon cornflour (cornstarch)

3 tablespoons icing (confectioners') sugar

* Frozen berries tend to be a little juicier so that's the route I'd take for these, but feel free to use fresh raspberries if you have them.

Blitz the raspberries and water in a blender until smooth. Strain out any seeds; you should be left with about 160 ml (⅔ cup) of purée. If not, add enough water to make it 160 ml (⅔ cup).

In the bowl of a stand mixer, pour 80 ml (⅓ cup) of the raspberry purée, sprinkle over the gelatine, and gently mix to make sure all the gelatine is in contact with the liquid.

In a medium saucepan combine the granulated sugar, corn syrup, salt, and the remaining purée. Cook over a medium heat, stirring occasionally, until the mixture reaches 115°C (240°F) on a sugar thermometer; this should take about 4–6 minutes.

With the mixer on low, slowly pour the hot sugar mixture into the gelatine raspberry mixture. Once it is all in there, kick up the mixer to a notch below the highest setting and let it go until light, fluffy, pale, and the bottom of the bowl that was hot is now barely warm – around 6–10 min. Add the vanilla extract and go for about 30 seconds more.

While this is happening you can prep the baking sheet. Mix the cornflour and icing sugar together in a bowl and set aside. Lightly grease a 20 × 20 cm (8 × 8 in) sheet, then sift in most of the marshmallow coating, making sure all the sides are lightly covered; it helps to sift a bunch in, tap the sides and bottom, and rotate the sheet. Reserve a couple of tablespoons of coating for later.

Once the marshmallow mixture is done, quickly scrape it into the prepared sheet and smooth it out. It's gonna be sticky but just deal with it and don't freak out. Once it's in the sheet and probably freakishly sort of smoothed out, sift a tablespoon of coating on the top. Boom. Congratulations, you've just made marshmallows.

Let the sheet sit out for at least 4 hours, probably closer to 6 just to be safe, then pop the marshmallows out onto a cutting board and carefully cut into 2½ or 4 cm (1 or 1½ in) squares using a sharp knife or a pizza cutter, or a small round biscuit cutter.

Once they're all cut up, toss in a large (1 gallon) zip-top bag, sift in the remaining tablespoon of coating and shake the bag to get all the sides coated. Store in the zip-top bag for up to 2 weeks.

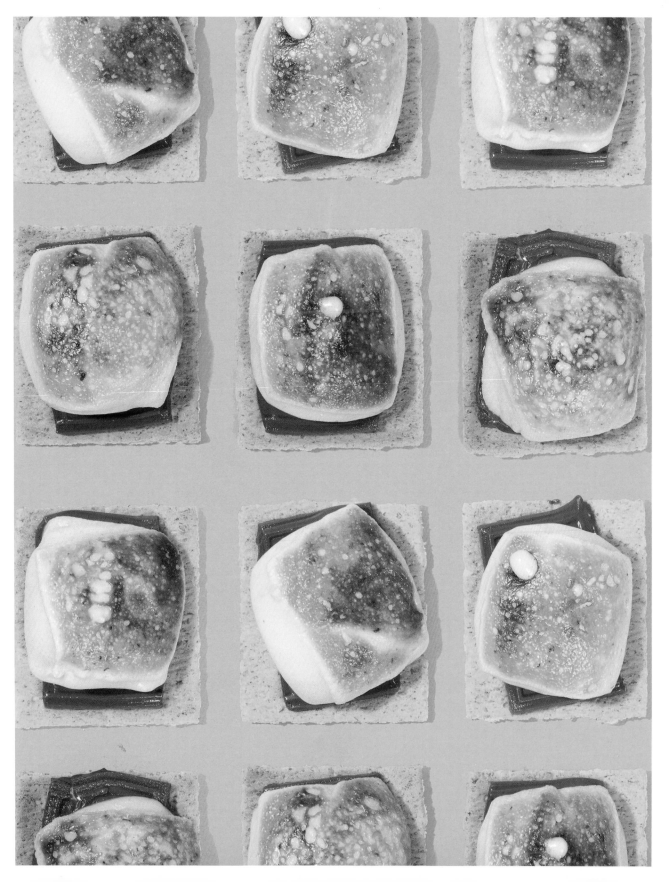

# FROZEN TREATS

When you live in Southern California like I do, it's pretty much summer all year round, which means I need something cold to eat 24/7. Enter Frozen Treats, where we talk about all the ice cream, sundae fundaes, and obviously popsicles. Yes, you need an ice-cream maker for the ice cream recipes, but it's a fun purchase and the quality's way better than anything in the store. Plus, how else are you gonna get cookies and salted caramel flavoured ice cream? If you don't have an ice-cream maker, there are still recipes for you: take your store-bought ice cream to the next level with my home-made sauces and toppings, or try my high-end popsicles. Summer will never be the same again!

# SUNDAE MAKERS

When it comes to ice cream I believe there's those destined to be enjoyed in a cone with some more complex flavours or add-ins, and then there are others, like vanilla buttermilk that are just really yelling, 'Hey, cover me in hot fudge, whipped cream and a cherry!' (see exhibit A, opposite). Here are some tips for the perfect ice cream situation:

1. Figure out the base: you can either go big with something hefty like a waffle or a slice of cake or even a scone, or you can just use some of the sauce to make a nice liquid bed.

2. Layer your sundae: you want goodness in every bite, so we take the nacho approach to the sundae, although maybe it's the sundae approach to the nacho? You always want to sandwich your ice cream with the sauce that's going on top. If you don't do this you'll have hot fudge sundae FOMO and spoonfuls will be absent of the sauce. Not ideal.

3. Top it with everything you want: I have whipped cream, sprinkles, and a cherry here, but you could easily just do the whipped cream or 10 cherries, or a giant handful of chopped nuts. Literally the sky (and maybe your stomach) is the limit.

## SIMPLE BUTTERSCOTCH SAUCE

### MAKES ABOUT 260 ML (1 CUP)

95 g (½ cup) lightly packed, light
  brown sugar

80 ml (⅓ cup) double (heavy) cream

90 g (⅓ cup) butter

1 tablespoon light corn syrup

¼ teaspoon sea salt (or coarse
  kosher salt)

1 teaspoon pure vanilla extract

Combine everything except the vanilla in a medium-sized saucepan and bring to a boil. Boil for 3 minutes, turn off the heat and add the vanilla. Cool slightly before using on waffles, ice cream, etc. Store in an airtight container in the fridge for up to 2 weeks.

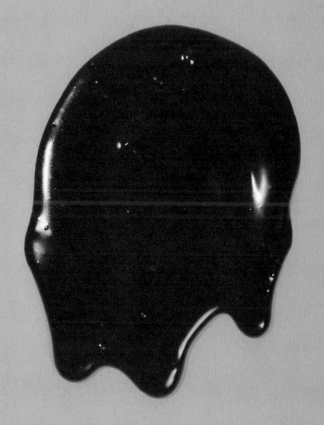

## HOTTEST FUDGE

### MAKES ABOUT 350 ML (1 CUP)

120 ml (½ cup) double (heavy) cream

100 g (3½ oz) good-quality dark
    (bittersweet) chocolate, chopped

2 tablespoons cocoa powder, sifted

2 tablespoons light corn syrup

pinch of salt

1 teaspoon instant coffee

Heat the cream in a medium saucepan over a low heat
to just below a simmer. Remove the pan from the heat,
add the chocolate, cocoa, corn syrup, salt, and coffee.
Let sit for 5 minutes to let the chocolate melt, then
whisk until smooth. Store in an airtight container in the
fridge for up to 2 weeks.

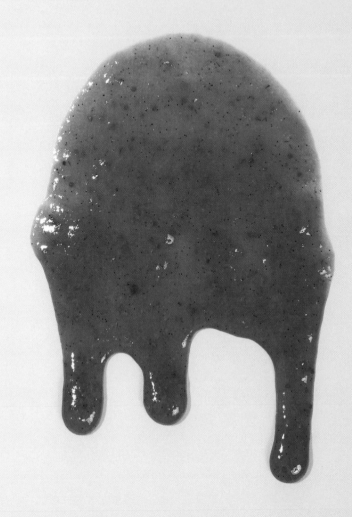

## VANILLA STRAWBERRY SAUCE

### MAKES ABOUT 350 ML (1 CUP)

450 g (1 lb) frozen strawberries, thawed

230 g (½ cup) white granulated sugar

120 ml (½ cup) water

1 vanilla pod, split, seeds scraped

pinch of salt

optional: 2 teaspoons orange liquor, such
as Cointreau or Grand Marnier

Combine everything in a medium-sized saucepan
(vanilla pod and seeds included) and bring to a simmer,
sort of smashing the berries as they heat. Simmer for
15 minutes until it's thick and syrupy. Cool slightly,
then mix in a blender for 30 seconds, until smooth.
If you want more of a syrup, don't blend, just run the
mixture through a fine mesh strainer. Store in an airtight
container in the fridge for up to 2 weeks.

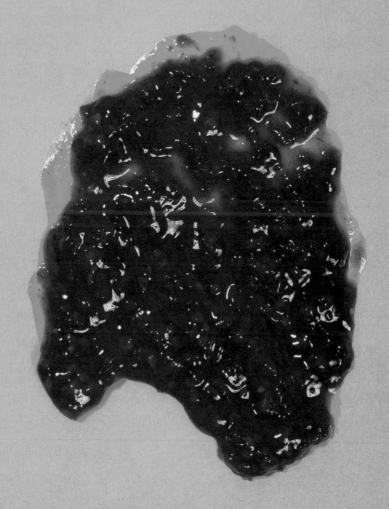

# BLACKBERRY BOURBON SAUCE

## MAKES ABOUT 350 ML (1 CUP)

350 g (12 oz) blackberries

80 g (⅓ cup) white granulated sugar

2 teaspoons bourbon

1 teaspoon pure vanilla extract

2 tablespoons water

1 tablespoon cornflour (cornstarch)

In a medium-sized saucepan over a medium heat, mash the berries and sugar together until the berries are broken down and the mixture starts to bubble. Meanwhile, mix together the bourbon, vanilla, water, and cornflour together in a small bowl. Add this to the pan. When the mixture starts to bubble, bring it back to a boil and cook for 1–2 minutes, until thickened. Store in an airtight container in the fridge for up to 2 weeks.

# MAPLE-GLAZED CORNFLAKES

## MAKES 60 G (2 CUPS)

*Sometimes you just need to get a little freaky with your sundae toppings. Enter maple-glazed cornflakes. A little smokey in flavour from the maple syrup, and the toasting in the oven makes the cornflakes nutty. They're the perfect thing to top a sweet sundae or accidentally eat an entire batch of by the handful. Don't look at me like that – just make a batch and see for yourself.*

60 g (2 cups) cornflakes

2 tablespoons pure maple syrup

pinch of flaky sea salt

Preheat the oven to 150˚C (300˚F/Gas 2) and line a baking sheet with baking parchment. Toss everything in a bowl to evenly coat the cornflakes, spread out on the baking sheet, and bake for 5 minutes. Stir and bake for another 3–5 minutes, until golden brown. Remove from the oven and cool completely before using to top sundaes or eat by the handful. Store in an airtight container for up to 2 weeks.

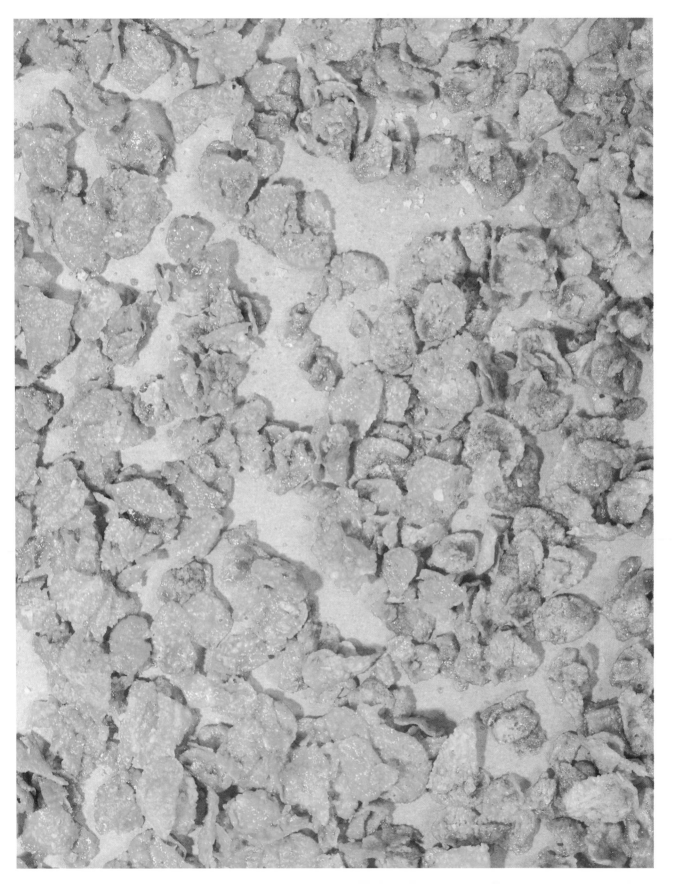

# VANILLA BUTTERMILK ICE CREAM

## MAKES 950 ML (1 QUART)

*Out of all the ice creams in this chapter, this is the most basic, and possibly my favourite. It's my little black dress of ice creams. I know you probably think this is gonna be gross because it's mostly butter-milk, but it might possibly be something to shout about from rooftops. It's tangy, not too sweet, and has just the right smack of vanilla. Just promise me you'll try it, okay?*

480 ml (2 cups) double (heavy) cream

pinch of salt

145 g (⅔ cup) white granulated sugar

1 vanilla pod, split, seeds scraped and reserved (or 2 teaspoons pure vanilla extract)

4 eggs

240 ml (1 cup) buttermilk

1 teaspoon pure vanilla extract

In a medium-sized saucepan stir together the cream, salt, and sugar over a low–medium heat. Heat just below a simmer and stir to make sure the sugar is dissolved. Add the vanilla pod and seeds to the warm cream, cover, and steep for 30 minutes.

Meanwhile, get your 4 eggs separated: yolks in a large bowl and beaten; whites set aside for whatever your heart desires.

Remove the vanilla pod, warm the cream up just a little bit more, then slowly pour half of that into the yolks while whisking. We're tempering the yolk so we have less of a chance of scrambled-egg ice cream. Pour the yolk mixture back into the pan and cook over a medium heat, stirring constantly, until the mixture reaches 77°C (170°F), or coats the back of a spoon and holds its shape when you run your finger through it (temperature is easier though).

Once it hits 77°C (170°F) pour through a fine mesh sieve into a large bowl, preferably something with a spout. Let it cool completely, add the buttermilk and vanilla extract, and churn the mixture in an ice-cream machine according to the manufacturer's instructions.

# COOKIES & CREAM 4 WAYS

## EACH ONE MAKES A LITTLE OVER 950 ML (1 QUART)

*A go-to for ice cream flavours for me is cookies & cream, but I also love cramming Oreos in all desserts possible. That's when I realised that there are not enough cookies & cream variations. Enter 4 different options: the Lindsay Lohan* Parent Trap *Peanut Butter combo, the Mint, the Coffee, and the Caramel. Each base is really good pre-Oreo of course, but you know the Oreo just takes them to another level.*

## & PEANUT BUTTER

240 ml (1 cup) double (heavy) cream

360 ml (1½ cups) whole (full-fat) milk

95 g (½ lightly packed cup) brown sugar

4 large egg yolks, beaten

185 g (¾ cup) organic, sugar-free
    peanut butter

330 g (1½ cups) crushed Oreos

In a medium-sized saucepan stir together the cream, milk, and sugar, then put over a low–medium heat. Heat just enough to dissolve the sugar, then slowly pour half of that into the egg yolks while whisking. Pour the yolk mixture back into the pan and cook over a medium heat, stirring constantly, until the mixture reaches 77°C (170°F), or coats the back of a spoon and holds its shape when you run your finger through it.

Once it hits 77°C (170°F) pour through a fine mesh sieve into a large bowl, preferably something with a spout. Whisk in the peanut butter, and let it cool completely. Churn the mixture in an ice-cream machine according to the manufacturer's instructions, adding the crushed Oreos 2–3 minutes before the ice cream's done churning.

# & MINT

360 ml (1½ cups) double (heavy) cream

360 ml (1½ cups) whole (full-fat) milk

pinch of salt

145 g (⅔ cup) white granulated sugar

4 large egg yolks, beaten

2 teaspoons peppermint extract

1–2 drops blue food colouring*

330 g (1½ cups) crushed Oreos

* You need blue because the yolks are yellow, so combining the two will make the mint colour. It's kind of like magic!

In a medium-sized saucepan stir together the cream, milk, salt, and sugar, and put on a low–medium heat. Heat just enough to dissolve the sugar, then slowly pour half of that into the egg yolks while whisking. Pour the yolk mixture back into the pan and cook over a medium heat, stirring constantly, until the mixture reaches 77°C (170°F), or coats the back of a spoon and holds its shape when you run your finger through it.

Once it hits 77°C (170°F) pour through a fine mesh sieve into a large bowl, preferably something with a spout. Whisk in the peppermint extract and food colouring, and let it cool completely. Churn the mixture in an ice-cream machine according to the manufacturer's instructions, adding the crushed Oreos 2–3 minutes before the ice cream's done churning.

# & COFFEE

360 ml (1½ cups) double (heavy) cream

360 ml (1½ cups) whole (full-fat) milk

pinch of salt

¼ cup coarsely ground coffee (I like a
   good medium roast for this)

145 g (⅔ cup) white granulated sugar

4 large egg yolks, beaten

330 g (1½ cups) crushed Oreos

In a medium-sized saucepan stir together the cream, milk, salt, and coffee, and put on a low–medium heat. Warm up the mixture to just below a simmer, then turn off the heat and cover. Let it steep for 10 minutes. Strain out the coffee grinds through a fine mesh sieve.

Once it's strained, add the sugar and heat until the sugar is just dissolved. Slowly pour half of that into the egg yolks while whisking.

Pour the yolk mixture back into the pan and cook over a medium heat, stirring constantly, until mixture reaches 77°C (170°F), or coats the back of a spoon and holds its shape when you run your finger through it.

Once it hits 77°C (170°F) pour through a fine mesh sieve into a large bowl, preferably something with a spout. Let it cool completely and churn the mixture in an ice-cream machine according to the manufacturer's instructions, adding the crushed Oreos 2–3 minutes before the ice cream's done churning.

# & CARAMEL

145 g (⅔ cup) white granulated sugar

2 tablespoons water

360 ml (1½ cups) double (heavy) cream

360 ml (1½ cups) whole (full-fat) milk

pinch of salt

4 large egg yolks, beaten

330 g (1½ cups) crushed Oreos

In a medium-sized saucepan melt down the sugar and water without stirring, only swirling the pan. Watch it go from the white sugar to a nice copper semi-fresh penny colour. Remove from the heat and add the cream and milk with the pinch of salt. The mixture will probably bubble up a little bit but don't be alarmed: it's supposed to happen. Just whisk it carefully until the lumps go away and the mixture is warm and smooth.

Slowly pour half of that into the egg yolks while whisking. Pour the yolk mixture back into the pan and cook over medium heat, stirring constantly, until the mixture reaches 77°C (170°F), or coats the back of a spoon and holds its shape when you run your finger through it.

Once it hits 77°C (170°F) pour through a fine mesh sieve into a large bowl, preferably something with a spout. Let it cool completely, then churn the mixture in an ice-cream machine according to the manufacturer's instructions, adding the crushed Oreos 2–3 minutes before the ice cream's done churning.

# BOURBON GINGERSNAP ICE CREAM

## MAKES 950 ML (1 QUART)

*We get to work a little magic with this ice cream by infusing our milk with gingersnaps to give a sort of warm flavour, then hitting it with a shot of bourbon at the end to make sparks happen. It's great by itself in a cone, but works just as well topped with butterscotch or hot fudge and whipped cream.*

230 g (2 cups) crumbled gingersnaps

500 ml (2 cups) whole (full-fat) milk

4 egg yolks

360 ml (1½ cups) double (heavy) cream

145 g (⅔ cup) white granulated sugar

pinch of salt

1 tablespoon bourbon

In a medium-sized bowl, stir the crumbled gingersnaps into the milk and set aside to soak for 1 hour. While that's happening we can make the rest of the base.

Get your 4 eggs separated, yolks in a large bowl and beaten, whites set aside for whatever your heart desires.

In a medium-sized saucepan stir together the cream, sugar, and salt, and put on a low–medium heat. Heat just enough to dissolve the sugar then slowly pour half of that into the egg yolks while whisking. Pour the yolk mixture back into the pan and cook over a medium heat, stirring constantly, until mixture reaches 77°C (170°F), or coats the back of a spoon and holds its shape when you run your finger through it.

Once it hits 77°C (170°F) pour through a fine mesh sieve into a large bowl, preferably something with a spout. Let it cool until the milk and gingersnaps are done making out. Strain the milk and measure to see if you have 370 ml (1½ cups). If needed, add a little more milk. Combine with the custard base and chill completely in the fridge. Once it's completely chilled add the bourbon and churn the mixture in an ice-cream machine according to manufacturer's instructions.

~~~~~~~~~~~~~~~~~~~~~~~~~~~~~~~~~~~~~~~~~~~~~~~~~~~

# ARROZ CON LECHE PALETAS

## MAKES 10 x 80 G (3 OZ) ICE POPS

~~~~~~~~~~~~~~~~~~~~~~~~~~~~~~~~~~~~~~~~~~~~~~~~~~~

*FROZEN. RICE. PUDDING. I know, it sounds kind of weird but it couldn't be more perfect. These cool dudes are creamy, not overly sweet, and every other bite you get some rice that's nice and chewy from the freezing. The recipe is dead simple too: just dump everything in a pan, babysit it for 30 minutes, then you've got rice pudding that's one step away from becoming greatness a.k.a. Arroz Con Leche Paletas.*

70 g (⅓ cup) jasmine rice

240 ml (1 cup) condensed milk

960 ml (4 cups) whole (full-fat) milk

½ teaspoon sea salt (or coarse
    kosher salt)

2 teaspoons pure vanilla extract

¾ teaspoon ground cinnamon

Combine the rice, both of the milks, and the salt in a medium saucepan. Bring the mixture up to a simmer over a medium heat, stirring pretty frequently to make sure none of the rice is sticking to the bottom of the pan.

Turn the heat down to low and simmer for 30 minutes, stirring frequently, until the rice is tender and the mixture has thickened slightly. Turn off the heat and add the vanilla and cinnamon. Now we've got some dynamite rice pudding, but we're taking it one step further and freezing it because I want to popsicle everything. Carefully pour the pudding into the popsicle moulds and let them cool to room temperature* before inserting the popsicle sticks and popping them in the freezer for 4 hours.

*If you freeze while the arroz con leche is still hot it can freeze at different rates and make it icy. Don't do dat.

# DULCE DE LECHE PUDDING POPS

## MAKES 10 x 80 G (3 OZ) ICE POPS

*Dulce de leche is the stuff dreams are made of. It's a sweet milk caramel that's just the best. Usually you can make your own by cooking down condensed milk but I always take the easy route and get a can of the pre-made stuff that's equally as good – all I have to do is open a can. These pudding pops come together super fast and I can't figure out if the hardest part is waiting for the popsicles to freeze or trying not to eat the leftover dulce de leche with a spoon.*

480 ml (2 cups) whole (full-fat) milk

¼ teaspoon sea salt (or coarse kosher salt)

2 tablespoons cornflour (cornstarch)

150 ml (⅔ cup) dulce de leche

In a medium-sized saucepan whisk together the milk, salt, and cornflour. Turn the heat to medium and whisk frequently until the mixture starts to simmer. Cook for 1 minute, whisking constantly, until the mixture's thickened. Whisk in the dulce de leche until it's smooth.

Carefully pour the pudding into the popsicle moulds and let them cool to room temperature before inserting the popsicle sticks and popping them in the freezer for 4 hours.

# STRAWBERRY CREAMSICLES

## MAKES 8 x 80 G (3 OZ) ICE POPS

*This is that popsicle you make when you see the most perfect strawberries at the supermarket. The strawberry flavour shines through in these bebes and goes perfectly with a warm summer's day.*

450 g (1 lb) strawberries, hulled
   and quartered
¼ cup white granulated sugar
½ cup double (heavy) cream
1 teaspoon pure vanilla extract
pinch of salt

Add the strawberries and sugar to a blender and blend for 30 seconds until smooth. Set aside.

In a medium bowl whip the heavy cream until soft peaks form, then fold in the strawberry purée with the vanilla and salt.

Pour the mixture into your popsicle moulds and freeze for about an hour before inserting the popsicle stick and freezing completely, for about 4 hours.

# DRINKS

Knock Knock
Who's there?
Refreshing drinks.
Hurry up and let me in,
it's really hot out here!

~~~~~~~~~~~~~~~~~~~~~~~~~~~~~~~~~

# GRAPEFRUIT MINT MARGARITAS

## BY THE GLASS OR THE PITCHER

~~~~~~~~~~~~~~~~~~~~~~~~~~~~~~~~~

*This drink for me is like the summer anthem of drinks. It's just as easy to make a pitcher as it is a glass so you can decide how many drinks you want to have to yourself. I know the mint addition might sound a little weird but trust me: grapefruit and mint were meant to make out and be refreshing.*

*For 1 drink*

5 mint leaves, plus extra sprigs to garnish

170 ml (6 fl oz) ruby red grapefruit juice*

45 ml (1½ fl oz) silver (blanco) tequila

1 tablespoon freshly squeezed lime juice

*For a pitcher*

30 mint leaves (about 1 bunch), plus extra sprigs to garnish

1 litre (4½ cups) ruby red grapefruit juice*

270 ml (9 fl oz) silver (blanco) tequila

90 ml (3 fl oz) freshly squeezed lime juice

*To serve*

ice cubes

1 lime, cut into wedges

sea salt (or coarse kosher salt), for rim

\* When it comes to the grapefruit juice, go ahead and just use a good-quality bottled one. Odds are you're using it to hydrate during the summer, when ruby red grapefruits aren't in their prime. Save some money, and save some hand work.

To make a single drink, muddle the mint leaves in the bottom of a shaker. Add the rest of the ingredients with a few ice cubes; shake vigorously. Use a lime wedge around the rim of the glass, then dip it into the salt. Add a few ice cubes to the glass, strain the drink in, and garnish with a baby-tree-sized sprig of mint and a lime wedge.

To make a pitcher, muddle the mint leaves in the bottom of a pitcher. Add the rest of the ingredients. Stir well, then use a slotted spoon to fish out the mint leaves. If serving right away then stir in a good amount of ice cubes, and serve in salt-rimmed glasses, garnished with the mint.

# STRAWBERRY CUCUMBER VODKA

## MAKES 375 ML (12 FL OZ)

*This stuff is like that fancy spa water except it's vodka and it turns the most insane colour of ruby red. It's a little sweet from the strawberries so you could easily just top a shot of it off with tonic or club soda, or use it in The Sunburnt Greyhound on page 169. Whatever you do, just make sure you constantly have it in the fridge for your summer drinking.*

260 g (1½ cups) strawberries, hulled and quartered

260 g (1½ cups) English cucumber, peeled and sliced

375 ml (12 fl oz) vodka

In a large jar with a tight-fitting lid, combine everything, give it a good shake, and leave it in a cupboard for 3 days. Shake it once a day to let it know you haven't forgotten about it.

After the 3 days, strain it out, put it back in said jar, and refrigerate until ready to use.

# THE SUNBURNT GREYHOUND

## MAKES 1 DRINK

*The classic greyhound is simply vodka and grapefruit juice. For my version, I've added a little colour by adding the Strawberry Cucumber Vodka on the previous page – think of it as the greyhound's cool older sister. Please drink responsibly and always wear sunscreen.*

55 ml (2 fl oz) Strawberry Cucumber
    Vodka (page 166)
170 ml (6 fl oz) grapefruit juice
juice of half a lime

*To serve*
ice cubes
½ grapefruit, sliced (optional)

In a shaker, add the vodka, grapefruit juice, and lime with a handful of ice. Shake for about 15 seconds until nice and cold. Serve over ice and garnish with a grapefruit slice or an umbrella or two.

~~~~~~~~~~~~~~~~~~~~~~~~~~~~~~~~~~~~~~~~~~~~~~~~

# HIBISCUS LIMEADE

## MAKES ABOUT 1.4 LITRES (1½ QUARTS)

~~~~~~~~~~~~~~~~~~~~~~~~~~~~~~~~~~~~~~~~~~~~~~~~

*Sometimes it's really hot out and you don't need something that might make you take your top off. Let me introduce you to limeade, or better yet, Hibiscus Limeade. It's similar to the Jamaica agua fresca you can get at a taqueria but with a greater lime influence. And if you thought I was just jumping ship on alcohol, you're wrong: there's a shandy on the next page.*

1.2 litres (5 cups) water

170 g (¾ cup) white granulated sugar

zest from 1 lime

20 g (¼ cup) dried hibiscus (sometimes labelled 'flor de Jamaica')

180 ml (¾ cup) freshly squeezed lime juice

*To serve*

ice cubes

1 lime, sliced (optional)

In a small saucepan bring 240 ml (1 cup) water and the sugar to a simmer. Turn off the heat, stir to dissolve the sugar if needed, and add the lime zest and hibiscus.

Let it steep for 15 minutes, then strain out the hibiscus and lime zest. Let that mixture cool completely then add the remaining water and lime juice. Refrigerate until nice and chilled. Served with ice cubes and slices of lime.

~~~~~~~~~~~~~~~~~~~~~~~~~~~~~~~~~~~~~~~~~~~~~~~~~~~

# HIBISCUS LIME SHANDY

## MAKES 2–3 DRINKS

~~~~~~~~~~~~~~~~~~~~~~~~~~~~~~~~~~~~~~~~~~~~~~~~~~~

*A shandy is usually just 50/50 beer and lemonade – a drink meant to be poured over you like that scene in Flashdance. And I love it. I decided to switch it up with the Hibiscus Limeade and haven't looked back. It's sort of like a sister-from-another-mister to The Beergarita. The hibiscus goes surprisingly well with the beer and the lime is just a given. I'd go with a lighter Mexican or wheat beer for a slightly stronger flavour.*

350 ml (12 fl oz) Hibiscus Limeade
  (page 170)
350 ml (12 fl oz) beer, either light Mexican
  or wheat beer

*To serve*
ice cubes
1 lime, sliced (optional)

Fill 2 or 3 large glasses with ice and fill halfway with the limeade, then the rest of the way with the beer. Garnish with the lime slices.

# THE BEERGARITA

## MAKES 1 PITCHER

*I mention The Beergarita above and figured it'd be rude to casually namedrop and not introduce you. If you're not down for making the limeade and needed something, like, 5 minutes ago, then this one's for you. Plus it makes a pitcher so you're ready for party mode.*

4 x 200 ml (12 fl oz) bottles of beer, either
  light Mexican or wheat beer
90 ml (3 fl oz) light agave
120 ml (4 fl oz) fresh lime juice

*To serve*
ice
1 lime, sliced (optional)

In a large pitcher, carefully stir together the beer, agave, and lime juice. Serve this over ice and garnish with lime slices.

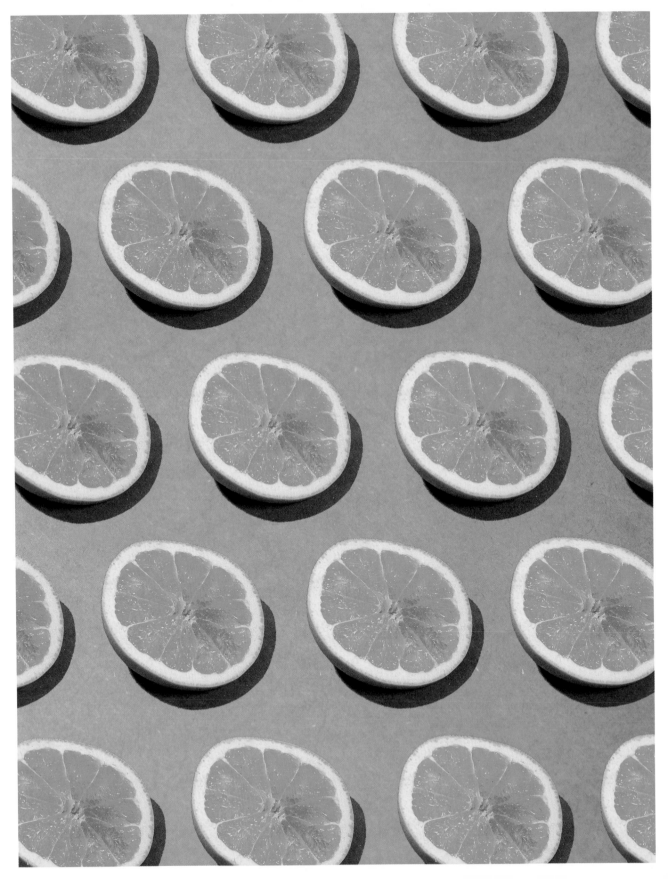

# PUNCH/DANCE

## MAKES ABOUT 2 LITRES (2 QUARTS)

*There's this thing I like to do called punch-dancing where I move around and sort of flail my arms in the air forcefully as if I'm punching the clouds. I like to think it burns calories while I wait for my food to cook, but if it's something you're not comfortable with this drink is sure to, uh, help with that. Serve with a lime wedge or a maraschino cherry, or be free and do both.*

960 ml (4 cups) pineapple juice

240 ml (1 cup) mango nectar juice

240 ml (1 cup) cranberry juice

juice of 2 limes

480 ml (2 cups) ginger ale

gin or vodka, optional

*To serve*

ice

1 lime, cut into wedges (optional)

maraschinio cherries (optional)

To make the punch, mix together everything except the alcohol in a large pitcher or punch bowl. You can either serve it straight up over ice with a wedge of lime and a maraschino cherry or add 25–50 ml (1–2 fl oz) of gin or vodka to the glass first.

# WATERMELON SANGRIA

## MAKES ABOUT 6 CUPS

*Sangria is probably my favourite vessel for eating fruit. If you use a red wine the fruit isn't really edible at the end, but with a nice light rosé, you'll want to maybe eat all the fruit first. Bring to a picnic to make lots of friends, if you're into that sort of thing.*

1 standard bottle of rosé

½ seedless watermelon, cut into 4 cm (1½ in) cubes

½ grapefruit, thinly sliced

4–5 strawberries, hulled and sliced

In a large pitcher add the rosé, half the watermelon, grapefruit, and strawberries. Stir to combine and chill in the fridge for at least an hour.

Take the leftover watermelon and place it in an airtight container or on a plate in the freezer. We're making watermelon ice cubes.

When you're ready to serve, fill glasses with watermelon ice cubes then top with the sangria. Garnish with the alcohol-infused grapefruit slices.

# FOR THE DOG

We've got two dogs, Nomi and Mose, that I might just love more than certain food groups (not carbs – that's too out of control). I like making them treats from time to time because they both love peanut butter, and it's the only borderline healthy thing that they like. Plus they need incentives if I'm ever going to be able to teach them how to dance.

# DOGGY FRO-YO

## MAKES 8–12, DEPENDING ON SIZE

*I know this probably sounds like a very Southern California 2007 thing, but dogs don't care what's cool and what's not – they just want to eat everything they see. Both my dogs love these and they're sooo cheap to pull together. You can stop at just the base recipe, or go ahead and top with a little more: try 50g (½ cup) blueberries or half a peeled apple for starters.*

250 g (1 cup) low- or non-fat Greek yoghurt

60 g (¼ cup) organic, sugar-free peanut butter

1 banana

2 tablespoons ground flaxseed

12 unsalted Pretzels (optional)

Place everything except the Pretzels in a food processor or blender and blend until smooth. Pour into an ice-cube tray, silicone mold, or muffin tin lined with cupcake liners (fill halfway with these so the treats aren't too much). Top with the Pretzels, if using, and freeze until soild.

# PUMPKIN FLAXSEED DOG TREATS

## MAKES 2–3 DOZEN, DEPENDING ON THE SIZE

*Now I know you're probably thinking that you could easily go out and buy your dog treats, but you don't even know what's in half of them. These things are super easy to throw together and it makes enough to try and make some friends. Brown rice flour is used because a lot of dogs seem to have a reaction to wheat. If that's not the case for your pooch, go ahead and sub some regular wholewheat flour in there.*

1 tablespoon ground flaxseed

5 tablespoons water

2 tablespoons organic, sugar-free
   peanut butter

125 g (½ cup) pumpkin purée

350 g (2 cups) brown rice flour

Preheat your oven to 180˚C (350˚F/Gas 4).

In a medium-sized bowl whisk together the flaxseed and water, then let it sit for 2 minutes.

Whisk in the peanut butter until completely smooth, followed by the pumpkin.

Add the flour and stir with a wooden spoon until the mixture comes together. Use your hands to kneed the dough, moulding it into a ball. If it seems too dry add an additional tablespoon of water.

Roll the dough out between 2 sheets of parchment paper to ½ cm (¼ in) thickness.

Use a cookie cutter or small biscuit cutter to cut out shapes, then place on a parchment-lined baking sheet. Re-roll scraps as needed: you should get anywhere from 24–36 treats, depending on the size of the treat.

Bake for 30 minutes, until lightly golden and dry to the touch.

Let cool completely before giving to your dog. Store in an airtight container for up to 2 weeks.

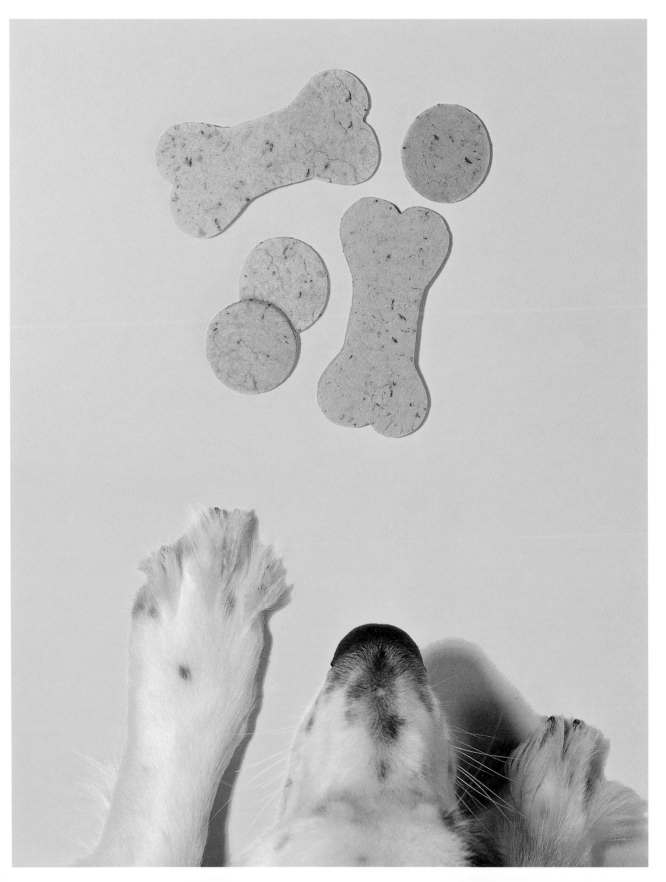

# NO-BAKE PEANUT BUTTER TREATS

## MAKES 18–20

*These are really good to make during the summer when you don't want to turn on the oven. They stay cool in the fridge and only use a few pantry staples, which means they're ready to make any time. Perfect for those treat emergencies that we all know happen when you can't give the dog the spaghetti you're eating.*

90 g (⅓ cup) organic, sugar-free peanut butter

90 g (⅓ cup) brown rice flour

1 tablespoon ground flaxseed

1 teaspoon honey

In a medium bowl mix together all the ingredients until well combined. Scoop out the treats with a melon baller or teaspoon, roll into a ball, then flatten with a fork or your thumb. Store in an airtight container in the fridge for up to 3 weeks or in the freezer for up to 6 weeks.

# MAKE IT YOURSELF

When it comes to making things myself instead of just buying them there are a few questions I have to ask: 'Is it cheaper to make it?' and 'Is it (that much) better than something I can just buy?' I mean, if I have to spend more money and put in more effort to make something that's just as good then I'm team store-bought, all the way. Good thing is, all the recipes in this chapter are either far superior, less money or a little bit of both. And maybe it'll save you from needing to put clothes on to go to the store. Maybe.

# STEAK SEASONING

## MAKES ABOUT 80 G (½ CUP)

*Steak seasoning is something I put on EV-ER-Y-THING. I love it on all meats, eggs, potatoes – I may have even considered it to be a cologne. The only issue I have is the unnecessary dyes and the price tag. It's almost always cheaper to make your own spice mix, and this one is no exception. It might seem like a lot of ingredients, but that's what makes the whole mix so flavourful. Find a grocery store with a bulk spice section to save yourself even more money.*

½ tablespoon dill seeds

½ tablespoon coriander seeds

1 tablespoon dried garlic flakes

1 tablespoon dried onion flakes

½ tablespoon chilli (crushed red pepper) flakes

½ tablespoon paprika

35 g (¼ cup) sea salt (or coarse kosher salt)

1½ tablespoon freshly ground black pepper

Crack the dill and coriander seeds by using a pestle and mortar, your pepper grinder on a coarse setting, or by gently thwacking them in a zip-top bag with a heavy pot.

Mix all the ingredients together in a jar or container that has a tight-fitting lid. This makes a lot but you'll probably be surprised at how fast you go through it. It will keep for around 3 months in an airtight container.

# TACO SEASONING

## MAKES ABOUT 160 G (1 CUP)

*Growing up, tacos were a constant in the house, and they always involved a pound of minced (ground) beef and a packet of taco seasoning. I still have that same craving, but I feel there's some flavour lackage with the packet one, so I went ahead and mixed up my own. It's perfect on the classic minced beef but it's also a really easy way to spice up a store-bought rotisserie chicken for an even quicker taco fix.*

6 tablespoons chilli powder

2 tablespoons ground cumin

2 tablespoons paprika

2 tablespoons dried oregano

2 tablespoons garlic granules

2 tablespoons onion powder

1 tablespoon ground coriander

1 tablespoon sea salt (or coarse kosher salt)

Mix all the ingredients together in a jar or container that has a tight-fitting lid. It will keep for around 3 months.

To use:

Brown 450 g (1 lb) minced beef in a frying pan, add 3 tablespoons of the spice mix and 80 ml (⅓ cup) water, and cook for 2–3 minutes, until most of the water has evaporated.

*or*

Take 350 g (2 cups) shredded rotisserie chicken and add 3 tablespoons of spice mix with 80 ml (⅓ cup) water and cook for 2–3 minutes in a large frying pan over a medium heat, until the mixture has heated through and most of the water has evaporated.

# EASY PIZZA DOUGH

## MAKES 2 MEDIUM-SIZED PIZZAS

*I think 95 per cent of people would agree that pizza needs to be an individual food group. There's all the melted cheese, a bunch of sauce, and, if you're like me, something spicy. I love making pizza at home because everything I want goes on there and sometimes it lets my freak flag fly. I'm sure this isn't the ultra-grand supreme of pizza doughs but it's also ridiculously uncomplicated and requires no kneading. It's a good recipe to dip your toes in the yeast water and it's perfect for pizza emergencies.*

350 ml (1½ cups) water

7 g (¼ oz) sachet active dried yeast

500 g (4 cups) white bread flour or
Tipo '00' flour

2 teaspoons salt

2 teaspoons white granulated sugar

3 tablespoons olive oil

First things first: make sure your water is the right lukewarm temperature – it's a sure-fire way to kill yeast if the temperature isn't correct. Use a thermometer and heat up the water between 38–43˚C (100–110˚F), or whatever the temperature on the packet of yeast says. This is probably not as hot as you think. Once you get the temperature down, sprinkle the yeast over the water and carefully mix it in. Let this sit for about 10 minutes.

Now's a good time to prep the rest of the ingredients: measure out the flour in a large bowl (or a large pot with a lid if you're me) and add the salt and sugar. Measure out the olive oil but don't add it quite yet.

After the 10 minutes you should be able to see little bubbles on the soaking yeast, and the liquid will be sort of murky; now we know the yeast has bloomed. Take this mixture and pour it all at once into the flour-salt combo. Stir with a large wooden spoon until the mixture comes together. Add the olive oil and use your hands to finish the dough in the bowl or pot, making sure it's all combined and the dough is just barely sticky. Yes, it's a wet dough – don't freak out.

Add a little oil to the bowl or pot to make sure the dough doesn't stick, then cover it with a lid or cling film (plastic wrap) and set in a warm, draft-free area for at least an hour. Ideally the dough should rest for 6–8 hours to really get a better flavour, so this would be perfect to make before work so it can rest all day and be ready for you when you get home.

When you're ready for your pizza, preheat the oven to 250°C (500°F/Gas 10), or as close to that as you can get, and grease and line a 28 × 43 cm (11 × 17 in) pan with foil. Don't use parchment unless you want a fire.

Top with whatever sauce, cheese, and toppings you fancy*, and bake for 10–12 minutes, until bubbly and golden brown.

*Obviously I have BBQ Chicken Pizza on page 56, which always has a special place in my heart, but there are a few close seconds:

> pesto x mozzarella x cooked crumbled breakfast sausage x sliced mushrooms

> hot wing sauce x mozzarella and crumbled blue cheese x grilled chicken x thinly sliced onions (scallions).

> classic tomato sauce x pickled jalapenos x pepperoni

# HOMEMADE CROUTONS

## MAKES 60 G (2 CUPS)

*Homemade croutons are one of those things that I think everyone needs to know about. The stuff you buy in the store is way overpriced and old, and that just can't happen to your mouth. Despite the amount of not-salads in this book, I actually eat a lot of salads at home, and when I do, these babies are sure to make an appearance. I haven't even looked at a box of rocks that pass as bread croutons in forever. Just do yourself a favour and make a little more than you think you need – you're gonna eat half straight off the pan.*

60 g (2 cups) bread*, cut into 2.5 cm (1 in) cubes

1 tablespoon olive oil

pinch of sea salt (or coarse kosher salt)

pinch of freshly ground black pepper

any other spices you want – I like some garlic powder, or even the Steak Seasoning (page 194) would be a nice twist

Preheat the oven to 180°C (350°F/Gas 4) and line a large baking sheet with baking parchment.

Place the bread cubes on the baking sheet, drizzle with the olive oil, add the seasonings, and toss together so it's evenly coated.

Bake for 10 minutes, tossing halfway through to make sure browning happens evenly. While they're still warm they'll be a little soft on the inside, which I love, and then they turn into not-tooth-shattering cubes of gold. Toss on any salad or soup you want

* Literally any bread you have in your kitchen can be a crouton. I looove a good nutty or seedy bread, but I've used just about all of them. Once I even used a couple of hamburger buns I had leftover from burger night.

# VANILLA EXTRACT

## MAKES 350 ML (12 FL OZ)

*Something that makes you feel like a super-wizard in the kitchen is making your own vanilla extract. There's something awesome about putting a couple of ingredients in a jar, waiting a couple of weeks, and having a large amount of something that's sold for a lot more in the grocery store. You can calm down about how expensive vanilla pods are because we're buying them in bulk online. There are a lot of different ratios out there for the perfect vanilla extract but I find the most important steps are carefully heating up the vodka – please don't ignite your kitchen! – and scraping the seeds, or 'caviar', from the pods; these couple of steps help speed up the process. I also make it in 350 ml (12 fl oz) batches so I can use old jars and bottles from vinegar, maple syrup, molasses, etc, which usually come in that size.*

350 ml (12 fl oz) vodka – it doesn't need to be top shelf; I like SVEDKA

4 × 15 cm (6 in) vanilla pods, split, seeds scraped and reserved

A clean and dried-out 350 ml (12 fl oz) container – go ahead and recycle any of the jars or bottles mentioned above

In a medium saucepan, carefully heat up the vodka over a medium heat until tiny bubbles start to form; you want it hot but not boiling. Whenever you're transferring the vodka – into the pan and then into the container – turn off any open flames and do it away from any heat.

While the vodka is heating up, add the vanilla pods and seeds to the container, folding the pods in half as you put them in to make sure they stay submerged.

When the vodka's nice and hot, use a funnel to carefully pour it into the container. Let it sit out until it's room temperature then date it with some masking tape and seal it up. Let it sit in a dark cupboard for at least 2 weeks, ultra-preferably 2 months, then strain and use it in whatever needs the liquid gold.

# BROWN SUGAR

## MAKES 880 G (4 CUPS)

*This is probably one of those things where you're like, 'Billy stop it, I'm not making my own brown sugar!' And before I made this I would've been with you in camp store-bought. But, I'm telling you, this is far superior to anything you can buy in the supermarket and it's almost half the price. When I originally made this it was out of necessity; but after realising it stays super soft even after a couple of months, I stuck to making my own. It never gets lumpy, never hardens up, and it's what I use to make anything with brown sugar in this book. Just promise me you'll try this out for yourself.*

880 g (4 cups) caster (superfine) sugar
115 g (⅓ cup) unsulphured (not
    blackstrap) molasses

This ratio gets you a nice golden brown sugar. If you need dark brown sugar, just go ahead and double the molasses.

To make, pour the white sugar in a bowl and make a tiny dent in the middle. Add the molasses and use an electric mixer to mix until it's completely combined. If you don't have an electric mixer, no worries. It's a bit of a workout for your hands, but mix the sugar and molasses together with a rubber spatula until it's roughly combined. Then use your hands to finish the job until no lumps of molasses exist and it's nice and fluffy – and you try your best to not put your face in it.

# INDEX

*(var.)* indicates a recipe which is a variation of the main recipe on the page given

# THANK YOU

Writing a book takes approximately a thousand people to properly birth it, but obviously I had a budget that allowed for, like 10. Even with that amount there's plenty of shouting out to do.

Steve, the man that has to deal with my twerking and baking fails and major coffee consumption on a daily basis: thanks for trying to keep me on track and telling me when things are shit, and for all the love you throw my way.

My mom and sister, both of whom helped out immensely with recipe testing and super supported me throughout this process.

My grandma, for cooking with me and answering the million questions I had about her Blackberry Cobbler.

Adrianna, my friend and fellow blogger, who helped guide me through the process and endured late-night with pictures of ice cream.

Mose and Nomi, the two dogs that can equally fill my day with happiness and anger but then somehow win me over with a thousand sparkly heart emojis, for eating every treat option I gave them and maybe spitting some out.

Ben Wagner, who felt my need for a kick-ass cover and said yes when I asked him to design some custom type.

And lastly to Kate Pollard and the team at Hardie Grant, thank you guys so much for giving me the opportunity to birth this baby into the world.

# ABOUT THE AUTHOR

Billy Green is the voice behind the blog *Wit & Vinegar*. He lives in Southern California with his partner, Steve, and their two dogs, Mose and Nomi, where he consumes way too much coffee and chocolate. If he's not cooking he's probably watching some television revolving around housewives or drag queens.

witandvinegar.com

Whip It Up! by Billy Green

First published in 2015 by Hardie Grant Books

Hardie Grant Books (UK)
5th & 6th Floors
52-54 Southwark Street
London SE1 1UN
www.hardiegrant.co.uk

Hardie Grant Books (Australia)
Ground Floor, Building 1
658 Church Street
Melbourne, VIC 3121
www.hardiegrant.com.au

British Library Cataloguing-in-Publication Data. A catalogue record
for this book is available from the British Library.

ISBN: 978-1-78488-002-6

Publisher: Kate Pollard
Senior Editor: Kajal Mistry
Art Direction: Billy Green
Copy editor: Zelda Turner
Proofreaders: Kaye Delves and Louise Francis
Indexer: Cathy Heath
Colour reproduction by p2d

Printed and bound in China by 1010

10 9 8 7 6 5 4 3 2 1